Chumash Renaissance

Chumash Renaissance

Indian Casinos, Education, and
Cultural Politics in Rural California

Paul H. Gelles

Solitude Canyon Press
Santa Barbara, California

ISBN: 1481176145

ISBN 13:   9781481176149

Library of Congress Control Number: 2012923153
CreateSpace Independent Publishing Platform
North Charleston, South Carolina

I dedicate this book to my wife, Iliana,
and to my children, Daniela and Darien.

Contents

Part II Culture and Education

Part III Working toward Understanding
and Reconciliation

Illustrations

Historical

Contemporary

Note to the Reader

In order to make this book more concise and reader-friendly, the support material, background detail, and sources for the information presented in the main text have been compiled into notes and placed toward the back of the book. These notes are organized by chapter and reference the paragraph in the main text that they support.

Throughout this book, I use the terms "Native American," "American Indian," and "Indian" interchangeably. When used in the context of the nineteenth century, the term "Hispanic" is used for individuals of Spanish and Mexican descent. When used in a modern context, "Hispanic" and "Latino" are used interchangeably and refer to individuals from Mexico and other Latin American states. The term "white" is used by me throughout this book to refer to Americans of northern European descent.

Because this book is not focused on the Chumash language, I have standardized the spelling of Chumash words, eliminating apostrophes and other phonetic symbols used to render their correct pronunciation. For the latter, see *A Guide to the Samala Language of the Ineseño Chumash People* by the Santa Ynez Band of Chumash Indians and Richard Applegate.

Chumash Renaissance

The image of 'rich Indians' is powerful and provocative. It challenges prevailing mainstream attitudes that have existed since colonial times, and which assume the inferiority of Native Americans... [For] the first time in this country's history, Native Americans are participating in corporate capitalism, becoming involved in party politics, and forcing the American public to take their demands and needs seriously. In short, financial profits have bought some Native Americans political, legal, and social power."

Eve Darian-Smith, *New Capitalists: Law, Politics, and Identity Surrounding Casino Gaming on Native American Land*

"So now with the money, we're able to talk to Forestry—and we have a voice! Before, you didn't. I could have been talking to the wall for the same answer I was getting from the Forestry or another government-to-government. Now we have more money. Now everyone wants a donation. Now our voice is heard. When you're poor and you're living in a shack, you have no voice! What happened during the California gold rush? They had all the gold. We didn't care about the gold! Now a hundred years later here, in a different form, we have our gold. Now we are being heard."

Adelina Alva-Padilla, spiritual leader of the
Santa Ynez Band of Chumash Indians

"The detractors of the Santa Ynez band will just have to be disappointed, I guess, that the natives are not just standing around, somehow nobly contemplating their 'plight' as a 'once proud people' or some other hogwash."

C. Cordero, guest editorial, *Santa Ynez Valley Journal*

"renaissance" rebirth... a movement or period of vigorous artistic and intellectual activity

Websters Dictionary

Preface

I am not a Chumash specialist or "expert," and this book is not a comprehensive, scholarly treatise of the tribe. Rather, it is a story about an important contemporary issue from a particular perspective, one that is informed by anthropology and by my work with the tribe and other indigenous peoples. The goal is to use historical and cultural reporting to provide insight into the cultural renaissance of the Santa Ynez Chumash, the opposition faced by the tribe, and the deeper historical currents and changing cultural politics of rural California.

In a book about the politically loaded topic of Indian casinos, education, and culture, it is important to be up front about the origins and basis of one's perspective. I came to know the Chumash in a round-about way. Coming of age in the Golden State during the late '60s and early '70s, I had no idea that California Indians were still alive. I was a fairly typical California kid, and any ideas I had about Indians came from John Wayne movies, "The Lone Ranger" TV show, visiting Indian ruins in the Southwest, and playing cowboys and Indians in the backyard. On screen and in books, American Indians were presented as either bloodthirsty primitives or as stoic, noble savages—*and always in the past*. The message received was that they and their way of life were long gone. There was absolutely nothing about California Indians in my high school, even though this was a time of native activism. Nor was there anything in popular culture to indicate that they were still with us.

College was not much different. Although I had a few chance encounters with Indians in the far North while attending Humboldt State University, the local native communities were largely hidden from view. Even the fairly visible Wiyot settlement on the way out to Table Bluff, poor and run-down with rusting cars in the yards, looked abandoned. Like other tribes in nearby Trinidad and Big Lagoon, the Wiyot were off the map—there were no signs marking their small "rancheria." However, I did learn of the 1860 massacre of a couple hundred Wiyot men, women, and children on Indian Island in the Humboldt Bay. Finding out about this and other atrocities, and reading about Ishi, who, way back in 1911, was considered the "last survivor of Aboriginal America," reinforced the idea that California Indians were pretty much gone.

My first exposure to indigenous society was outside of California. After a year of college, I traveled overland to Panama and then went on to Peru, where I encountered a strong and vital native culture in the Andes. Here were millions of people speaking an indigenous language, Quechua, one that had been the common language of a large empire, the Inca. I was fascinated, to the point that I spent the next twenty-five years doing anthropological research, and publishing and teaching, about indigenous societies in the Andes and Latin America.

Yet during this time I still knew little about native California and nothing about the Chumash. Although I was a frequent visitor to the Santa Ynez Valley, where my parents had moved in the early 1980s, it was a long time before I was even aware that there was a reservation in the valley. As in northern California, American Indians were pretty much off the map.

I first visited the reservation while attending a concert there in the mid '90s. Surprised to find native people staffing the casino, which was still in a large tent at that point, I realized how little I knew of local indigenous history and culture. I knew there was a mission, that many roads followed old stagecoach routes, and that the Danes had established the settlement of Solvang in the early 1900s. These parts of the region's heritage were well advertised and enshrined in local celebrations such as Danish Days and Santa Ynez Day. But Chumash heritage was absent in public displays: there were no museums or statues, no welcoming signs in Chumash (as there were in Danish), no festivals or civic celebrations marking the aboriginal presence in the valley—just the newly established and impermanent white tent of the casino.

As the new casino was being planned, I began to hear and read negative comments. I was surprised by the tone. Some of the valley elite were up in arms about the impending development, and I heard people say things like, "Chumash speak with forked tongue," that they were "Indian givers," that they were "destroying the valley," that they were "bad neighbors." Yet other locals were supportive of the Chumash. In strong contrast to my research on the poor but numerous Andean peoples, the Chumash were relatively few in number but quickly gaining considerable economic and political power. I decided that I needed to learn more about the indigenous people in my own backyard.

The opportunity to do so arose when I moved my family to the valley on a permanent basis in 2003. The tribe's education committee and newly hired education director were trying to get a summer program off the ground, and I was brought on as a cultural coordinator and counselor. While working closely with Chumash families in the program, I made friends and learned about the effects of the casino revenues on their lives. Working again in the Chumash summer program in 2004 and 2005, I also tutored and mentored Chumash youth. And in the summers of 2005, 2007, and 2008, I received outside grants to carry out research on the effects of the casino funds on Chumash education and culture.

Working with the tribe, while rewarding, has not always been easy. The tribe is rightfully wary of outsiders, and while some outsiders have played a positive role in Chumash cultural survival, others have not. After several years of my proving myself a friend of the tribe, more and more people opened up to me. As made clear in the acknowledgments at the end of this book, I have learned a great deal from the Chumash, and I appreciate their trust.

At the same time, working for the tribe has turned my experience as an anthropologist on its head. Rather than being funded by universities and foundations to research and teach about poor and relatively powerless indigenous peoples in Latin America, I was now employed by an American Indian tribe. Today, because of the casino revenues, the Santa Ynez Chumash have the resources to recover and protect their cultural and historical patrimony. Far from the general practice of anthropology, it is the native peoples *themselves* who are funding research and using anthropologists, linguists, and historians to understand their own history, strengthen their identity, and get back what has been taken from them. The casino revenues have been decisive in this process.

The renaissance of the Chumash is part of a larger process taking place in many areas of rural California. I recently took my family on a trip back to Humboldt County, where the native presence in the area was invisible to me during my college years there. Thirty years later—as in Santa Ynez and across the state—Indians in Humboldt are literally on the map. The rancherias today are well marked on Highway 101, some have small casinos, and the Indians there now have a visibility and political and economic clout that was impossible to imagine thirty years ago. Most striking is the Table Bluff Wiyot tribe, which, instead of living in the run-down shacks I used to see, now lives in new homes on their relocated rancheria.

As we drove back down Highway 101 from northern California to the Santa Ynez Valley, I was struck by the number of tribes we passed, tribes that have been there all along but that just recently appeared on the map, large roadway signs now announcing their rancherias and reservations. These new signs point us not only toward the physical territories of a thriving people but to deeper economic, political, and cultural processes at work in rural California today.

Paul Humphreys Gelles, Los Olivos, California, 2013

Introduction

"The tribal opponents think we should still be living in *tule* huts and weaving baskets for a living. This is the hand we've been dealt. We didn't want it this way, but now we're playing it the best we can."

Chumash descendant in his thirties

"The past is never dead. It's not even past."

William Faulkner,
Requiem for a Nun

Chumash Empowerment and the Politics of Culture

This book is about a particular place and its people, past and present. The Santa Ynez Valley, located thirty miles north of the city of Santa Barbara in California, is the ancestral homeland of the Samala people, better known as the Santa Ynez Band of Chumash Indians, today a "casino tribe." The Santa Ynez Chumash have achieved remarkable educational gains since the mid-1990s because of the casino revenues, and these revenues have also helped intensify a cultural renaissance that began in the late 1960s. A good part of my book concerns the tremendous cultural and linguistic rebirth, as well as strengthening of identity, that has taken place over the last few decades. While this is tied in part to the tribe's newfound economic and political power, it also emanates from the past, a past which is very much still alive for the Chumash.

Identity is also tied to place, and the Santa Ynez Valley is a beautiful place. Its hills are covered with sere dry scrub, manzanita, oak forest, and meadows that turn an emerald green in the spring with stunning

1

wildflowers adding a mix of colors. During "peak green," California poppies and lupin shimmer in gold and blue patches among the scrub brush or along lush green pastures framed by yellow blankets of invasive mustard. Coming over the San Marcos Pass above the area known as Paradise on the recently renamed "Chumash Highway," one has an expansive view of oak savannahs, mountains, and Lake Cachuma.

Sloping downriver from the lake and the Santa Ynez River watershed toward Lompoc, the Santa Ynez Valley encompasses the towns of Santa Ynez, Solvang, Los Olivos, and Buellton, as well as the smaller community of Ballard. The neighboring areas of Gaviota and Los Alamos also share much of the same landscape and general culture. With an overall population of some twenty-five thousand, the valley is a wonderful place to live, with a small-town feel, safe neighborhoods, and a great climate.

The valley is culturally diverse—though it is usually not represented as such—and, for the most part, people get along well. On the surface, there appears to be little conflict among different ethnic groups, primarily whites, Latinos, and Chumash (there are few Asians and African-Americans). In my experience, as well as that of my Chumash and Latino friends, many close friendships and marriages cross ethnic lines in the valley.

Yet almost all the Chumash and Latinos I know have also experienced racism at one time or another in their lives here. So, too, there are cultural misunderstandings among different groups in the valley, often the result of a lack of knowledge about the other groups' cultures, values, and life ways. Many of the tensions beneath the surface came bubbling to the top when the Chumash began to gain power and develop their new casino in the late 1990s.

Opposition and Response

The Santa Ynez Band of Chumash Indians, made up of some hundred and fifty members who have more than twelve hundred descendants, is the only federally recognized Chumash group and thus the only group permitted to operate a casino. The casino is located on the 128-acre reservation thirty miles north of the city of Santa Barbara and is one of the largest casino resorts between Los Angeles and San Francisco. As a result of it, the

Chumash have prospered and have quickly become a major political player and economic powerhouse in the Santa Ynez Valley and in Santa Barbara County.

This current position is in marked contrast to their experience in the last two hundred years, during which the Chumash were poor and marginalized by dominant groups, enduring successive waves of colonization by Spain, Mexico, and the United States. This sad and tragic history, which is reviewed in part one, makes the economic, political, educational, and cultural gains over the last couple of decades that much more remarkable.

Although supported by many local residents, the Chumash have faced and still face stiff opposition from others. Eve Darian-Smith, who has written about the construction of the Chumash casino in the early 2000s, finds the image of "rich Indians" to be powerfully provocative, bringing to the surface prevailing mainstream assumptions, attitudes, and stereotypes about Native Americans. This was clearly revealed by the opposition to the tribe of a small but wealthy and vocal Concerned Citizens group, part and parcel of a nationwide backlash against the installment of Indian casinos.

This and other local groups—such as POLO (Preservation of Los Olivos) and POSY (Preservation of Santa Ynez)—made up of celebrities, wealthy ranchers, and everyday citizens, have since fought the Chumash over other issues, including the permitting of alcohol in the casino's restaurants, annexation of 6.9 acres to build a cultural center and museum, development of fourteen hundred acres of rural land east of town, and naming a major thoroughfare of the valley the "Chumash Highway."

While these groups have legitimate concerns, their critiques of the tribe are often misguided and misinformed. A great deal is revealed when we look at how opponents of the tribe often attack the tribe personally, perpetuating stereotypes and misinformation, and studiously ignoring key facts. My book exposes their assumptions and critiques their critiques by looking at the larger cultural politics of the valley and the region.

Are the Chumash living in the exact same way as their ancestors did? No, of course not. Are they perfect human beings living in a perfectly harmonious native society? Again, no. Have there been conflicts within the tribe and between different Chumash groups? In fact, yes. Have the Chumash stumbled at times in moving from being a dirt-poor reservation to a prosperous nation running a twenty-first-century casino, a resort, and many other enterprises? Again the answer is yes.

And yet, as detailed in the chapters ahead, the tribe has done a great number of things right, such as establishing important businesses that will support the well-being of Chumash descendants for generations to come; developing and taking pride in their culture, and educating themselves and others about their heritage; providing far-reaching educational opportunities for over twelve hundred Chumash descendants; establishing a well-used tribal clinic that helps the low-income residents of the valley, thus supporting the local businesses, homes, and ranches that depend on them; cooperating with other Chumash and American Indian groups to strengthen their identities; and contributing a great deal to the valley's inhabitants in regards to culture, education, and the economy.

Yes, there are social costs to Indian casinos, but, at least in the case of the Chumash, there are also clear gains. Besides the usually touted jobs, cultural events, and tourist dollars, there is the great benefit of having better-educated Indian people with a greater sense of their history, identity, and culture, a culture that was forcibly extracted and denied to them.

Indigenous Communities and Sovereignty

My perspective on the Chumash is rooted in the larger context of the problems and prospects facing indigenous groups throughout the Americas. Who exactly are we talking about? The United Nations' definition is as follows:

> Indigenous communities, peoples, and nations are those which, having a historical continuity with pre-invasion and pre-colonial societies that developed on their own territories, considered themselves distinct from other sectors of the society now prevailing in those territories, or parts of them. They form at present non-dominant sectors of society and are determined to preserve, develop, and transmit to future generations their

ancestral territories and their ethnic identity, as the basis of their own continued existence as peoples, in accordance with their own cultural patterns, social institutions, and legal systems.

The Chumash fit this definition well and thus have a lot in common with the more than 45 million other indigenous people in the Americas.

Yet, despite their large numbers and the large territories indigenous people control, national and popular discourses throughout Latin American, Canada, and the United States denigrate, marginalize, or altogether erase indigenous identities. This is true whether we are speaking of countries with large indigenous majorities, such as Peru, Bolivia, and Guatemala, or in others with a small percentage of indigenous people, such as Brazil. Until recently, native peoples were treated as legal minors and denied voting rights in many countries, and the word "Indian" or "indio" is routinely used as an insult, usually meaning "backward" and "stupid." Indigenous civilizations, cultures, and their contributions to contemporary society are ignored or presented as belonging to the past with no relevance to today's world. The great majority of indigenous peoples throughout the Americas form part of the underclass and have fewer economic opportunities, a lower standard of living, poorer health, and reduced life expectancy than the majority of citizens in the countries in which they live.

An important consideration for our discussion is that national governments throughout the Americas assign a different legal status to indigenous communities, whether they be called native communities, *reservas*, reservations, *comunas*, *comunidades indígenas*, or *comunidades campesinas*. These communities control millions of acres of land throughout the Americas, and, with some variation, they usually possess some form of sovereignty, that is, official status as legal entities with jurisdiction over the natural resources, membership, and customary law in their territories.

The relationship of the United States government with its indigenous people is just one variation of a relationship found in countries throughout the Americas. To understand the casinos tribes, then, we have to understand the particularities of "sovereignty" in the United States. This, in turn, helps illuminate why the US casino tribes have prospered and today have more economic strength, political clout, and possibilities for greater self-determination than their indigenous counterparts elsewhere in the Americas.

First dealt with as preexisting tribal nations with their own governments by the European settlers, federally recognized tribes are today understood as domestic, sovereign, self-governing nations who enjoy *a nation-to-nation relationship with the US government*. France, England, and the United States entered into treaties with native groups over such things as hunting and fishing rights, and they were treated as sovereign nations with self-government and jurisdiction over their own lands. Indian tribes today are governments with certain powers and separate rights recognized by the US Constitution and the Supreme Court. As the "First Peoples," Indian tribes thus have a different legal and political status than other "minority" groups. *The immigrant, ethnic group model applied to other hyphenated Americans thus does not apply to these First Peoples, who are citizens of preexisting nations.* Indeed, American Indians have dual citizenship as US citizens and as members of their tribes.

Yet not all tribes have the right to operate casinos; only those that are federally recognized do. Thus, there is an important legal difference between the more than five hundred and fifty federally recognized tribes and other tribes within the United States. The Santa Ynez Chumash are one of these five hundred and fifty tribes, and it is their federal recognition—and the voters of California—that has allowed them to have a casino and to make the educational, political, and cultural advances detailed in this book.

By the nature of their attacks, it is clear that most opponents of the Chumash do not understand the ways that the concept of sovereignty became politically established through Supreme Court decisions and acts of Congress, rather than through some caprice of the Chumash. To be fair, the historical reasons and legal reality behind casino tribes' special relationship to the United States government are poorly understood by the general public. In high schools and even universities, students are exposed to little information about tribal sovereignty and related political issues. Thus, most California residents are unaware of the reasons American Indians have special rights and are not the same as other immigrant ethnic groups.

But it is precisely the legal existence of these rights and native sovereignty that has brought prosperity to the Chumash and many other formerly impoverished American Indians. In that regard, one can only marvel at the political and economic gains of the casino tribes, bright lights in an otherwise opaque geography of relative poverty that stretches from Tierra del Fuego to Alaska and encompasses tens of millions of indigenous people. Whether we are talking about Peru, Brazil, Argentina, Guatemala, Mexico, Colombia, the United States, or Canada, most Indians occupy the lowest social rung in terms of education, health, and income. Even in those countries where native peoples have achieved political clout through indigenous movements, such as in Ecuador and Bolivia, that power has not translated into economic mobility—Indians there remain, on the whole, very poor. And so, from north to south, east to west, all across the Americas, the casino tribes of the United States, such as the Chumash, are the clear exception to the rule.

In sum, although Chumash society today is radically different from that of indigenous societies in Latin America, they share a common historical experience involving colonization, subordination, and racism, as well as resistance to these. Yet, unlike their Latin American counterparts, the Chumash today—because of the particularities of Indian policy in the United States—are overcoming their long history of political, economic, and cultural marginalization.

The Politics of History and Identity

At the core of my book is a story about colonialism and about the past poverty and social, political, and educational marginalization of the Chumash people in the Santa Ynez Valley. It is also the story of the advent of their casino, how they overcame the forces allied against them, and how they are currently providing a range of opportunities for their children. Part of the story is about cultural loss, cultural survival, and the revitalization of Chumash identity. Along the way, we will look at the larger historical and current sociopolitical context and interethnic relations in the valley. This larger context frames current Chumash educational and cultural initiatives, as well as opposition to and critiques of the tribe. The book ends by reviewing these critiques and offers suggestions for reconciliation.

While critiques of the Chumash get a lot of attention, many local residents, including those who support the tribe, are unaware of the progress the tribe has made, educationally and in strengthening their culture, community, and health. As one tribal member told me,

> The community doesn't know about our programs, even though it's no secret that we have set up these programs to help our children. But we have not disclosed much information to the public. We're doing something for our children without bragging about it; we're proud of our kids but most tribal people are modest and that's a good thing. I learned since living here bragging is not who we are. And although we have some issues with certain kids, it's no different than the outside community. Some people I know who live outside the reservation have heard a lot of negative things, that kids are running wild on the reservation. When I mention our program and our graduates, they seemed surprised and ask, 'Why aren't you saying this? It needs to be told.'

In sum, there is an important story that has been little reported and that should be told. There is a real need for the valley residents, and the residents of California as a whole, to understand the great bounds and leaps in Chumash and Indian education and cultural revitalization that have been set in motion by the casino revenues. Indeed, it is hard to keep abreast of the many cultural projects and educational programs that are being developed.

Yet it is also important to anchor the many benefits from the casino in the past. Everything begins with culture. Several Chumash firmly explained to me that although the casino revenues have given the tribe power over its cultural patrimony and the opportunity to create new cultural projects, it was in fact the preexisting culture that made the casino and its advances possible. "Without culture, none of this would have happened," says Desi Zavalla, a burly, pony-tailed Chumash man in his forties, pointing in the direction of the casino and nodding toward the improved reservation houses within view. The culture was already there; it was just more covert, more private, and family-driven. Desi and others grew up learning stories, songs, and doing ceremony long before the casino was built.

But, today, the resources are available to pursue cultural activities *on a collective level* that was heretofore unimaginable. Indeed, the tribe now has the resources to revitalize its language, safeguard Chumash cultural patrimony, support public ceremony and remembrance, and sponsor cultural programs for adults and youth.

A major goal of this book is to document this cultural revitalization and the ways in which the Chumash tribe is now becoming an equal participant in the cultural development of the whole region. By presenting a different view of the cultural makeup and politics of the area, I also hope to get residents here and elsewhere in the state to reconsider recent history and the native peoples who live here, as well as the cultural diversity that generally flies under the radar in many parts of rural California.

Part I

History and Politics

One

Early Chumash History and the Creation of White Culture in the Santa Ynez Valley

"Clearly the Chumash fared no better in their freedom than they had under the bondage of the mission system. They had merely changed masters."

Bruce W. Miller, *Chumash:*
A Picture of Their World

To understand why education and cultural revitalization are so important to the Santa Ynez Chumash, we must look to history. This larger history is also necessary for understanding the cultural politics in the valley at present. We will see that the Chumash were triply colonized, and each wave of colonization had important consequences for Chumash identity today. Studying major historical shifts in the valley allows for an understanding of how certain social groups—and not others—have become memorialized in local celebrations at present.

Chumash Villages at the time of the Spanish Invasion. Drawing by Emma Munger. Location of village sites based on Gamble 2008:71.

The Chumash Peoples: Early History and Culture

The word "Chumash" comes from the word for shell bead money that was produced on the Channel Islands, and the word was first applied to the island dwellers. The Spanish colonizers extended this term to the different indigenous groups occupying the territory between what today is Malibu (*Humaliwu*) and the southern Salinas Valley. The Chumash were one of the most populous native California groups, with approximately twenty-five thousand people living in some one hundred and fifty villages, and they controlled one of the largest territories. Each village had its own chief, who represented his group with other native groups and with the European invaders alike, and this form of leadership continued through the mission period of the early nineteenth century.

The large amount of historical and archeological literature about the Chumash shows that in pre-contact times there was a general cultural complex shared in a culturally distinctive way by the inhabitants of this region. This included common adaptations to coastal and inland habitats, hunting, gathering (especially acorns), fishing, and a fiesta system of feasting and trade between different chiefs and their villages. Besides being excellent hunters and fishermen, the Chumash produced stone cookware and finely woven baskets. Young women left their home villages to marry and settle in their husbands' villages. These ties and the wide-ranging social and economic networks managed by the chiefs speak to a complex society. The general world view was multifaceted, with well-developed esoteric understandings and sophisticated rites managed by ritual specialists, as well as great knowledge about plants, animals, astronomy, and other scientific domains.

We now look at the general Chumash colonial experience throughout what today are Ventura, Santa Barbara, and San Luis Obispo Counties, before turning to the "Samala" people or "Ineseños," that is, the Chumash of what today is the Santa Ynez Valley.

Colonization of the Chumash

Cabrillo was the first European to have contact with the Chumash—in 1542, he encountered them in wood plank canoes along what today is the Ventura and Santa Barbara coastline. But the Chumash were basically left alone by Spain for the next two hundred years; Alta California was on the periphery of the Spanish colonial system.

Rafael Solares (1822-1890), chief of the Ineseño community at Zanja de Cota, posing in traditional dancing regalia. Based on a photograph of him taken by a French anthropologist in 1878. Drawing by Emma Munger. Information about photo from Black Gold Cooperative and Johnson 1997.

But during the last few decades of Spanish colonialism (late eighteenth and early nineteenth century), the Chumash territory was a strategic site of occupation, with five out of the twenty-one missions in California being established on Chumash territory. Santa Ynez, established in 1804, was the last of the five missions, following La Purísima, Santa Barbara, San Luis Obispo, and San Buenaventura. The Spaniards were interested in securing this relatively large group for labor and to keep the Chumash out of the hands of the Russians, French, and English, who were also making forays on this coast.

While some Indians joined the missions of their own will, many were brought in as indentured servants when the Spaniards burned their villages and forcibly converted them to Catholicism. The cross was buttressed by the sword. Once they entered the mission, they could not leave. Not only the fundamental labor supply for the mission system, the Chumash were also "farmed out to local settlers and soldiers as a labor force for which the mission was paid in return."

In contrast to the viceroyalties of Mexico and Peru, which had large peasant populations whose labor was readily on tap, Alta California was a remote, sparsely populated outpost in Spanish colonial America. Nevertheless, disease and the mission system took a large toll on native life. The population declined dramatically, from approximately twenty-five thousand in pre-contact times to around fifty-six hundred in 1805, and down to around twelve hundred in 1832. By the time of the first California state census in 1852, the Chumash numbered fewer than six hundred. This population decline of over 90 percent truly had the proportions of a holocaust for the Chumash.

Yet the population decline of those counted as "Chumash" can also be attributed to the Chumash suppressing their Indian identity as a means of survival. Being an "indio" in Spanish colonial America and under independent Mexican rule brought no advantages; along with African slaves, the *indio* was at the bottom of the colonial hierarchy. Their language, religion, and general culture were denigrated. Despite cultural pressures, the language persisted, and traditional religious specialists continued Chumash ceremonial life through much of the nineteenth century, although in a much abbreviated and clandestine form.

With Mexican independence came another wave of colonization. Like indigenous peoples throughout the Americas, the Chumash fared much worse after independence. As abusive as the mission system was, the Chumash during Spanish colonialism remained a distinct cultural group and were afforded some protection by the mission from the predatory owners of haciendas and ranches. With secularization of the missions in 1833 and the Mexican government's seizure of church lands, that protection was lifted in order to grant "freedom" to the Chumash and other native groups throughout the former Spanish colony. The "freedom" granted by the Mexican government in fact led to less freedom and greater disruption of Chumash kin networks and traditional ways of life—and, no matter, the Chumash still were forced to work without pay for the Presidio of Santa Barbara. While Chumash culture declined during the Mexican period, the surviving Chumash people lived near mission sites or were absorbed as ranch hands.

The final stake in the heart of early Chumash culture came with the third wave of colonization—the Gold Rush and California's incorporation into the United States in the mid-nineteenth century. Throughout much of California during this time, as statehood and the gold rush brought about the first massive immigration ever in the state, there was a bounty on Indian scalps. Some fifty thousand Indians throughout the state were annihilated within a few short years. Generalized racism toward Indians forced the Chumash to shed their language and culture to survive; they became even more dispersed, working largely as hired hands on local ranches.

As with indigenous groups throughout the Americas subjected to cultural and political pressure to abandon their identities, many Chumash individuals were forced "to pass" (as Mexicans) in order to survive. The Chumash today are aware of what their ancestors went through and the reasons for cultural loss. As former Chumash Public Relations Executive Director Frances Snyder says in reference to Chumash, "This isn't exactly a lost language. It was a forbidden language during the missionary period in California. Americans were even worse than the Spanish. It wasn't a very pleasant experience being an Indian in this country, so the Chumash stopped speaking their language and focused on Spanish, trying to pass as Hispanics."

A Valley on the Periphery: The Samala People under Spanish and Mexican Rule

At the time of the Spanish invasion, the Samala people (Ineseño Chumash) were made up of both smaller settlements and several large villages with a hundred to two hundred people in each, such as at Kalawashaq, Xonxonata, Soxtonokmu, Shahuchu, and Naxuwi. Besides the *aps*, or reed huts, the Chumash lived in, the Chumash settlements in what today is the Santa Ynez Valley often had dance compounds, ceremonial enclosures, playing fields, sweat lodges, and cemeteries.

But what stands out when looking at the valley against the flow of history is just how relatively small and isolated its populations have been and how it has always existed on the periphery of the different states of which it was part. Even in pre-contact times, and although the valley had several large villages, there was a much greater population concentration on the coast. The large coastal villages often had over two hundred, and some with as many as eight hundred, individuals. These served as both meeting place and economic hub between the Chumash of the Channel Islands and the interior groups (including those of the valley). Larger displays of status and trading occurred in the coastal communities. In sum, the small settlements and dozen or so larger villages that existed in the Santa Ynez Valley in pre-contact times constituted a periphery of sorts.

During the Spanish colonial period, the valley remained on the periphery. For two hundred years after their first foray into Chumash territory, the Spaniards ignored Alta California, preferring to concentrate on their other dominions. When they did colonize the area in the waning years of empire, it was through small missions and settlements that could barely be described as "towns" (*pueblos*). In contrast to the great centers of indigenous civilization in Mexico and Peru, each of which had large cities, divine kingships, and huge peasantries that had been easily yoked to Spanish colonialism two centuries before—yielding up Spanish-style cities with large cathedrals and universities in the sixteenth century—Alta California was sparsely populated at beginning of the nineteenth century. "Chumash villages dotted the coastline, and the pueblo of Santa Barbara was no more than a ramshackle collection of huts clustered around the Presidio."

And the Santa Ynez Valley was on the periphery of this periphery! There were three main trails—that is, Chumash footpaths—into the valley over the south-facing Santa Ynez Mountains, a formidable barrier to different forms of transportation for the next century. While El Camino Real went through the Gaviota Pass and was able to accommodate wagons only after the 1850s, the San Marcos Pass went from being a footpath to a mule trail in 1800, later becoming a major thoroughfare for the region.

Mission Santa Ynez was truly an outpost in a wild place—wolves, grizzly bears, and mountain lions abounded in the valley. The mission was founded in order "to effect the conversion of the remaining Chumash population in inland areas" and to provide support for, and a strong link between, the mission in Santa Barbara and Mission La Purísima in what today is Lompoc. The spot chosen for Mission Santa Ynez was the Chumash village of Alajulapu, which had good water and fertile fields for crops and grazing animals. These fields became the namesake "sunny fields," or *solvang*, of the Danish settlers a century later. The Indians at the mission in the early 1800s raised wheat, barley corn, beans, and other crops; dressed hides of animals; extracted tallow for candles; and wove cloth.

In the first half of the nineteenth century, Mission Santa Ynez *was* the valley, meaning that the Indians and their Spanish and then Mexican overlords (the few administrators, priests, and soldiers living there) constituted pretty much the entire populace. At this time, few other Spaniards or Mexicans lived outside the mission. Some Chumash retreated to the back hills and evaded mission rule, but their numbers were small. Nor were there any land grants or *ranchos* in the Santa Ynez Valley until well after Mexican independence and the secularization of the missions.

As we saw above, the Chumash population in general, from 1805 to 1852, declined almost 90 percent. So it was, too, in the case of the Santa Ynez Valley. A 1798 survey counted some twelve hundred Chumash in fourteen villages, but by 1856, that number had declined to just 109 individuals. So, around the year 1800, there were only about twelve or thirteen hundred people in the whole valley. By 1850—and mostly because of diseases such as typhoid, diphtheria, smallpox, influenza, and measles, which decimated the overall Chumash population, including that of Santa Ynez—there were only a hundred or so Chumash left.

Life was harsh. Several different indigenous people—such as the Chumash and non-Chumash, such as the neighboring Yokuts—had their villages burned to the ground and their populations brought into the mission at Santa Ynez. From the colonial period on, the valley "Chumash" were in fact made up of a mixture of ethnic groups.

Yet, as we will see in later chapters, some Ineseño culture survived and most of the Santa Ynez Chumash today can trace their descent directly to particular families that were living in the large villages of Kalawashaq and Soxtonokmu, the latter of which was the last standing Chumash village in the valley. In 1804, its people were forced to abandon their rich hunting grounds and trading networks for forced service and life at Mission Santa Ynez. The forefathers and -mothers of the contemporary Chumash had a hard time in Mission Santa Ynez. Along with Indians brought in from the Santa Barbara and La Purísima missions, they actually built the mission itself, and by their labor they maintained the predatory priests, soldiers, local ranchers, and, ultimately, the colonial system in general. But there was resistance.

One instance is the Chumash revolt of 1824, which began at Mission Santa Ynez. The reasons for the revolt are disputed—one version has it that there was a rumor that the Spaniards were going to massacre the Indians, while another is that a Chumash man visiting from another mission was flogged—but it is clear that mistreatment and coercion of the Chumash had gotten much worse a few years before the revolt. Whatever the reason, the revolt spread to Mission La Purísima and Mission Santa Barbara. After a pitched battle in Santa Barbara between some three hundred Chumash men and the Spanish military stationed at the Presidio, the Chumash fighters joined their women and children who had fled inland to the San Joaquin Valley, along with fugitives from the other two missions.

The physical coercion and brutality that underlay the colonial system and its religious indoctrination and claims of cultural superiority came to the surface during this conflict. The mission soldiers sacked the Indian dwellings and murdered several Indians whom they came across and who were not involved with the conflict. Two military expeditions were sent out to do battle and force the fugitive Chumash back to the missions. While many returned along with some of the local Yokut Indians, several hundred Chumash remained in the San Joaquin Valley.

The first land grant in the Santa Ynez Valley was given in 1836 in the area of Las Cruces, near the Gaviota Pass, where trails to the valley and to Mission La Purísima converged. In the years to follow and through 1846, when the United States took California (it was not formally annexed until 1848 under the treaty of Guadalupe Hidalgo), several more Mexican ranchos were granted in the valley, including Saca, La Laguna, Alamo Pintado, San Carlos de Jonata, and Corral de Quati. But these large ranchos, each of which spread over thousands of acres of land, "resembled simple homesteads more than the rich estates of popular imagination."

Although a couple of Chumash men received short-lived ranchos, and other Chumash received smaller tracks of land to cultivate, most took work as vaqueros, laborers, domestic servants, or in the trades they learned at the mission for the "people of reason" (*gente de razón*)—that is, the non-Indian population. Post-mission life led in a couple of instances to Chumash cultural revitalization, but it also led to continued cultural disintegration, alcoholism, prostitution, and incarceration.

In sum, four key points can be made about the experiences of the Santa Ynez Chumash during Spanish and Mexican rule. First, Spanish control of the Santa Ynez Valley was tenuous and short-lived, two decades at most. Second, the Mexican ranchos came late, were few and far between, and were also short-lived. Third, the Mexican period was characterized by the continued disintegration of Chumash society and great mortality through disease. No longer living together under the relative protection of the missions, most Chumash were scattered throughout the ranchos and "fared no better in their freedom than they had under the bondage of the mission system." Fourth, first during Spanish then Mexican colonialism, because the total population of the valley was small, the Santa Ynez Chumash constituted a significant percentage of the overall population. Indeed, the ranchos probably helped stabilize the Indian death rate. As is well documented, many of these individuals retained and transmitted cultural knowledge about Chumash ways of life.

Meet the New Boss: Changes in the Valley under United States Rule

The valley continued to be on the periphery, this time of white settlement in California, for the first few decades after California was annexed by the United States in 1848. This was largely because of the rugged Santa Ynez Mountains, which were "the only barrier in the road systems already existing between San Francisco and Los Angeles." Prior to 1868, the valley was largely outside the stage network and "did not have a road that even the sturdiest mud wagon could traverse." These same mountains would later hinder the completion of the railroad between Los Angeles and San Francisco.

In 1855, the final Santa Ynez Chumash families who had remained were forced off of the mission and their allotted lands; they settled a few miles away at Zanja de Cota, which was on land owned by the Church. That land was later acquired by the US government to become the Santa Ynez Indian Reservation. Continuing the process fostered by secularization, these Chumash worked largely as farm hands, vaqueros, and domestic servants after California became a state.

But the situation of the ranchos changed dramatically after California achieved statehood. Once California was annexed to the United States, the Land Act of 1851 made it difficult for the Hispanic grant holders to retain title. Heavy rains followed by a prolonged drought in the early 1860s decimated the ranchos and their cattle holdings. Out of these developments, a new pattern of ranch ownership and management emerged.

As one source nicely puts it,

> By the beginning of the 1870s, nearly all of the original rancheros had sold out to wealthy Yankees who brought fresh vitality and new financial resources to invest in the restoration of the ruined ranches. The land grant ranches, most of them broken up into more manageable holdings, gradually regained their viability. Herds were rebuilt, adobes remodeled and modern ranching and farming methods replaced traditional pastoral ways. Although the conversation in the bunkhouse remained in Spanish, in the *casa grande* English was spoken.

In this new ethnic hierarchy, Indians remained at the bottom, and they and their culture came under even greater assault. The gold rush and US takeover of California led to an even more retrograde view and treatment of the state's native inhabitants than under Spanish and Mexican rule, with the outright massacre of many indigenous inhabitants, especially in the north. Increased pressure was being exerted against the Chumash to hide their culture and pass as Mexicans.

This is backed by the testimony of the elderly daughter of one of the large ranch owners of that time. Jane Hollister Wheelright discusses the "Yankee" degradation of the Indians in her memoir of growing up in nearby Gaviota on the sprawling Hollister Ranch, previously part of the Spanish land grant Nuestra Senora de Refugio. "Buying out the Spaniards, by then under the Mexican flag (and perpetuating the tragedy), they accelerated the demise of the Indian population. My grandfather was one of them." Her own father, who was born in 1870, belonged to "a generation that despised Indians."

In 1859, a network of stagecoach roads in the Santa Ynez Valley began to be surveyed and developed at public expense to "augment the private thoroughfares, which were little more than ox-cart tracks linking the various ranchos." Of the three passes into the valley, San Marcos was chosen as the least difficult and was developed for stage traffic; soon after, the Gaviota Grade and Pass were developed, allowing access to the wharf at Gaviota Beach. These roads were built with the help of Chinese road workers (often called "coolies"), who graded the roads with picks, shovels, and wheelbarrows.

For the next several decades, until 1901, the stage, which was supported by US mail contracts, ran from Santa Barbara through the San Marcos and Gaviota Passes to Las Cruces, Ballard, and Los Olivos, and from there to Lompoc and Los Alamos. Matteis Tavern, built in Los Olivos in 1886, became a key link in the stage line from Santa Barbara to the train routes further north.

Yet the train's arrival from the north and its final stop in Los Olivos in 1887 had a huge impact on the valley, greatly accelerating "white" (sometimes called *gringo*, Anglo, or Yankee) settlement in the late nineteenth century. Photographs from the time of the Los Olivos train warehouse and lumberyard reveal a large enterprise, with eight-horse-hitch wagons hauling grain from nearby farms. These farms employed more "modern" agricultural techniques than in previous times, with twelve-mule-hitch dry farming in the valley bottoms and flat lands. Several of the Chinese, having built the railroad and graded Los Olivos's streets as they had the stage road in an earlier period, stayed on as cooks or established laundries.

The valley towns began to grow quickly, spurred on by the arrival of the train line from the north to nearby Los Alamos in 1882. That same year, the town of Santa Ynez was founded near the Chumash settlement at Zanja Cota when the church sold off land. A small land rush ensued. In anticipation of the extension of the Southern Pacific Railroad through Santa Ynez to Santa Barbara, 160-acre parcels were offered. Twenty-nine buildings were constructed in the first year alone. Santa Ynez and Los Olivos did boom in the 1880s, with saloons, blacksmith shops, pharmacies, barbershops, and merchandising stores.

But local hopes for a train route through Santa Ynez were dashed when, in 1901, the train connecting Los Angeles and San Francisco was built along the coast, not through the valley's difficult San Marcos Pass. Stage service continued between Los Olivos, Santa Ynez, the Gaviota wharf, and the new Danish colony of Solvang (established 1911) until 1914, when the old stagecoaches were finally put out of business by the Model T Ford. In a word, the rerouting of the train away from the valley effectively halted local growth. Had the train come through it, the valley would be quite a different place today.

Increasing Settlement in the Twentieth Century

The foregoing shows that when the Chumash Reservation was established at the turn of the twentieth century, the valley's population was still very small. Even with the influx of white settlers, people of Chumash descent, often employed as ranch hands and workers (as were local Mexicans), remained a significant percentage of the population. Yet, those living at the relocated village of Zanja de Cota—which became the Santa Ynez Indian Reservation in 1901—consisted of just a small number of extended families. What happened to the Santa Ynez Chumash and their reservation in the twentieth century is reviewed in the next chapter. Here, the focus is on the larger social context that developed in the valley during that time.

At this time, Los Olivos and Santa Ynez were just tiny communities. For example, there were only thirty-nine students in Los Olivos School at the turn of the century. Neither Solvang nor Buellton yet existed; there was just the extensive Buell ranch, the twenty-six-thousand-acre Mexican land grant of San Carlos de Jonata that R.T. Buell had acquired in 1872. Las Cruces was "a stagecoach stop located at a Y intersection where the Santa Ynez Valley and Lompoc Valley converged on the way to the Gaviota

Wharf." Gaviota was the closest port to the Santa Ynez Valley, a day's jour-ney. "With only horse-powered vehicles as an alternative in the 1800s, most of the surplus crop was hauled here in wagons."

Almost the whole valley, then, was still open country, made up of large and small ranches that abutted the Los Padres National Forest, established in 1907. And yet, although the population of the valley was small, it was also diverse. Besides the significant numbers of Chumash and Mexicans who were already there, and the growing number of white settlers, there were also the Chinese road and rail workers. Pictures kept by local ranching families and published in local histories show a mix of people, including white ranchers and Mexican and Chumash ranch hands.

The influx of Danish settlers in 1911 added another flavor to the eth-nic mix. That year, eighty-three Danes came from seven different states in United States to establish a colony dedicated to the preservation of Danish culture. These settlers bought almost ten thousand acres of land, corre-sponding to the eastern portion of the Buell ranch. The new settlement of Solvang was established next to the old mission, on which restoration had begun in 1904. It was also at the crossroads for the road that led to Lompoc and another to the wharf at Gaviota. Building materials for this Danish settlement came from the wharf or by train to Los Olivos. Early photos reveal nothing Danish about the town's architecture; rather, it looks like other pioneer western towns.

Yet the Danes kept a distinct identity. Until 1935, shopkeepers were required to speak Danish, and there was an annual cultural event celebrat-ing traditional Danish dances, songs, and plays. "Some of the locals from the surrounding towns probably attended these early events, but for the most part they were hard to follow because all of the singing and speaking was in Danish."

The automobile had a major impact; by 1928, the streets of Los Olivos, Santa Ynez, and Solvang had all been paved. Buellton, between the 1920s and 1940s, was better known as a destination than Solvang. The same could be said for Las Cruces, which, as we have seen, had been a stagecoach stop. In the late nineteenth and through the mid-twentieth centuries, because of its proximity to Gaviota pier, Las Cruces became a little village and later a stopover for automotive traffic. Nearby Gaviota State Park was established in 1927. Although Las Cruces is now gone, it used to be an important entryway into the valley.

The valley remained rather sedate until the World War II. The population of the valley—the towns of Solvang, Santa Ynez, Buellton, and Los Olivos, and surrounding ranches—was still just a few hundred people. In 1925, only eleven women and four men graduated from Santa Ynez Union Valley High School. In 1930, the census population was just 107 in Buellton, 193 in Los Olivos, 244 in Santa Ynez, and fifty-one on the "Indian Reservation."

After World War II, especially with the publication of an article about Solvang in the *Saturday Evening Post* entitled "Little Denmark," the valley began to change. The postwar automobile culture was in full swing, and tourists began flocking north from Los Angeles. The Danes "capitalized on the attention by developing an annual celebration called Danish Days" and the residents began incorporating Danish architectural style into their shops. A travel explosion brought thousands to Solvang and to Pea Soup Andersen's in Buellton as "car crazy Californians took to the open road and discovered the Santa Ynez Valley." Today, there is still a sizable population of people of Danish descent. Although the new generations speak little Danish, the culture is proudly celebrated in the annual Danish Days festivities.

The population of the valley increased steadily after 1970. In the '70s and '80s, people from Los Angeles and elsewhere discovered the rural tranquility of the valley. Its towns grew, as did the number of hobby ranches. This trend increased greatly through the '90s, with many celebrities and others buying small and large estates in the area. So, too, a growing number of commuters to Santa Barbara began settling in the relatively less expensive towns of the valley. And although the valley has had a Mexican presence for the last two hundred years, increasing numbers of Mexican migrants (and other Latinos) came there in the late 1970s and thereafter.

The combined population of the valley towns and outlying areas is still relatively small, around twenty-five thousand, and the local public high school graduates around three hundred students a year. Yet, despite its small size, there are great economic differences, from wealthy celebrities and ranchers to poor Latino farmhands and white service sector workers. There are a number of large ranches, each with thousands of acres that have been in the same families for generations. Many smaller ranches varying in size from five to a hundred acres are also found in the valley. These contrast greatly with low-income apartments in Buellton and Solvang. As we will see in the chapters ahead, social class figures importantly in valley life.

***

To sum up this chapter, we have seen that the Santa Ynez Valley was, until fairly recently, sparsely populated, fairly isolated, and on the periphery of the different larger societies of which it has been part. The original inhabitants, the Chumash, a strong people with a sophisticated society, lost control of their land and their destiny as they were physically and culturally assaulted by three successive waves of colonization. Although cultural transmission of Chumash life continued through some individuals, much was lost as people of Chumash descent had to suppress their language and identity to survive. While some moved to Santa Barbara and elsewhere, others remained on the reservation at Zanja de Cota Creek in Santa Ynez.

The valley was a diverse place in the early twentieth century, with Chumash, Mexican, Chinese, as well as Danes and other white settlers. Since that time, the valley's western heritage—its ranching culture, stagecoaches, and railroads—and its Danish heritage have been celebrated and enshrined in museums and civic events. But what about the Chumash, the first inhabitants of the valley, the descendants of whom are still with us? What happened to them and their culture over the last century, and why is it not celebrated locally?

Established in 1804, Mission Santa Ynez was the key institution for the early colonization of the Ineseño Chumash. Photo courtesy of the Santa Ynez Historical Society.

Gaviota Pass is one of three routes to the Santa Ynez Valley through the rugged Santa Ynez Mountains. These mountains proved to be an obstacle to the development of the stage network, and later the railroad, between San Francisco and Los Angeles. Photo courtesy of the Santa Ynez Historical Society.

Built in Los Olivos in 1886, Matteis Tavern was a key link in the stage line from Santa Barbara to the train routes further north. Much of the building material for the town of Santa Ynez and later Solvang came through Los Olivos. Other materials were shipped to the Gaviota Wharf and hauled over Gaviota Pass. Matteis was recognized as a historical landmark in 2010. Photo courtesy of the Santa Ynez Historical Society.

Some of the early white residents of the newly established town of Santa Ynez, late nineteenth century. Photo courtesy of the Santa Ynez Historical Society.

Pedro Lopez, Chumash cowboy. After the secularization of the missions, many Chumash men were absorbed into local society as ranch hands and cowboys. Photo courtesy of the Santa Ynez Historical Society.

Tom, Chinese cook at Mrs. Greers in Santa Ynez. Chinese laborers helped build the stage coach roads, the railroad, and the town of Los Olivos. Many stayed on as cooks and launderers, adding to the ethnic diversity of the valley. Photo courtesy of the Santa Ynez Historical Society.

Agricultural workers with Chinese cook, late nineteenth century. The train's arrival to Los Olivos in 1887 helped accelerate white settlement in the valley as well as larger agricultural enterprises in the valley bottoms and flat lands. Valley growth was curtailed in 1901 when the train connecting Los Angeles and San Francisco was built along the coast, bypassing the valley. Photo courtesy of the Santa Ynez Historical Society.

While this photo is labeled "Santa Ynez High School, 1896," it apparently includes the entire student body of the town at this time. There are a lot more brown faces, children of Chumash and Mexican descent, in Santa Ynez than in a school photo from Los Olivos this same year. Photo courtesy of the Santa Ynez Historical Society.

Maria Solares, standing on the right between two children, and Rafael Solares, on the left in a bear costume, with an unidentified woman, at Zanja de Cota, around 1889. Maria would become anthropologist Harrington's principal Ineseño informant and a major culture hero to the Chumash today. Photo courtesy of the Santa Ynez Historical Society. Information about photo from Black Gold Cooperaitve and Johnson 1997.

Ineseño Chumash women at Zanja de Cota, 1900. By this time, because of cultural pressure, the Chumash spoke mostly Spanish and dressed like other Mexican residents of the valley. Photo courtesy of the Harrington Papers, National Anthropological Archives, Smithsonian Institution 91-31414. Photo by Tulita de la Cuesta. Information about photo from Black Gold Cooperative and Johnson 1997.

Francisca Solares, a direct descendant of an Ineseño Chumash chief, surrounded by laundry at the old College Hotel in Santa Ynez, 1906. Photo courtesy of the Harrington Papers, National Anthropological Archives, Smithsonian Institution 91-31306. Photo by Cristina Moller. Information about photo from Black Gold Cooperative and Johnson 1997.

The adobe house of Francisca and José Solares at Zanja de Cota, 1906. Photo courtesy of the Harrington Papers, National Anthropological Archives, Smithsonian Institution 91-31505. Photo by Cristina Moller. Information about photo from Black Gold Cooperative and Johnson 1997.

José Dolores Solares, who was the chief of the Ineseño Chumash, around 1907. Photo by Mamie Goulet, courtesy of the Santa Ynez Historical Society. Information about photo from Black Gold Cooperative and Johnson 1997.

Solvang School, 3ʳᵈ through 5ᵗʰ grades, 1938. Established next to the old mission in 1911 by Danish settlers coming from other parts of the United States, Solvang added another flavor to the ethnic mix of the valley. Photo courtesy of the Santa Ynez Historical Society.

Two

From Powerless to Powerful: The Chumash in the Twentieth Century and Today

"Many years ago, our tribal members used the Unity Shoppe services in times of need, and the Unity Shoppe was there for us. We are thankful for the support and are very fortunate to be able to give back and help Unity assist families in our community."

Kenneth Kahn, Chumash business committee member

The Chumash in the Early and Mid-Twentieth Century

The Santa Ynez Band formerly tied to the mission was officially recognized by the federal government on December 27, 1901. It is one of the smallest Indian reservations in California, with only 127 acres. In the early twentieth century, some five or six extended families lived on the reservation; a 1930 census counted fifty-one people there. Even in the 1960s, the population living on the reservation was still small.

Yet the reservation has also always served as a place for short or extended visits by other Chumash living off-reservation in the valley working as ranch hands and domestics or living in the surrounding areas of Lompoc and Guadalupe, the Five Cities area, Santa Barbara, Los Angeles, and elsewhere. The strength of the mission ties and continued residence on reservation lands at Zanja de Cota Creek gave these Chumash families a distinct identity within the valley, while, culturally and biologically, there was much intermixture with the Mexican population, as well as with other groups, such as Filipinos.

The Santa Ynez Band remained, for the better part of the twentieth century, a poor and marginalized populace within the Santa Ynez Valley and Santa Barbara County. Listening to the personal narratives of Chumash individuals who lived both on the reservation and off-reservation gives a strong sense of just how marginalized the community was and the toll that linguistic and cultural suppression took on identity. One also gets a sense of the great lack of economic and educational opportunities.

The narrative about the "old days" recounted by Tonie "Chuca" Flores, born in the mid-1940s, is worth considering at length. Tonie, a tribal elder, grew up on the reservation. She and her ex-husband, Pete Zavalla, who is of Comanche descent, played an important role for over forty years in promoting Chumash culture and instilling native pride. She also became an amateur historian in the process and has in-depth knowledge of the tribe's past. Keeping with the pattern discussed in the previous chapter, Tonie's Chumash mother lived with a Mexican man of Spanish stock from Colima, Mexico. Tonie grew up speaking both Spanish and English, listening to both *Rancheros* and *Motown*. "I loved the music, the *Rancheros*, but I knew where I was from. Even though there was the Spanish food, speaking Spanish, going to Mexico to visit family, we'd come back to where we belonged, and that was on the Reservation."

Tonie moved to the reservation in 1957. Before then, ranchers often provided homes for their farm workers, but when that housing was no longer available, Tonie's great-uncle Chicho told her mother to come live on the reservation. Tonie's dad at first resisted the move because he knew it would be difficult, with no water, electricity, or gas. But he worked hard bettering the place and pumped water from the creek to their forty-five-foot trailer home so that they could shower and wash clothes and dishes. For their drinking water, Tonie says, "We would go to Santa Ynez, at the gas station there at Edison and 246, owned by the McNeelys, and they said that the Indians could get fresh water in five-gallon bottles to drink."

Her tone turns serious and angry:

> That was one of the things that really bothered me as a young girl. I would come and do homework with a kerosene lamp, and my mom would get in the car and drive to get water. And one of the things that I couldn't understand, why is it that you'd cross

Highway 246 to the gas station—the gas station had water, gas, and light—and then you'd cross over to the reservation and the reservation had no water, gas, or light. So the world over here on the Rez was a good world, and yet we didn't have the comforts of what they had across the street, and that was water, gas and light.

The tribe's relative lack of power again comes through loud and clear. As Mrs. James Pace was quoted as saying in the late 1960s,

> The county board of health has warned us again that we are in danger of epidemics of diarrhea or other illnesses if we continue to use irrigation water. Most of us buy bottled water to drink. If one of our neighbors uses water to irrigate with, no one else on the reservation can get a drop of water for sanitation or any other purpose until he's finished irrigating.

The general neglect from the public sector as well as the government handouts that arrived to the reservation in the form of welfare, surplus food give-outs, and the like (local merchants would donate toys and clothing to Chumash youth each year at Christmas) underscore the poverty of many Chumash. The reservation was like a Third World country, education board member Dominica Valencia told me. "At that time we had the Good Samaritans come in, you know, the ones that go to Mexico and all over? And they'd come in every three months and do our teeth, an exam, do what they could do, the minimum. We really were just dependent on everybody's charity; whoever could come in and offer help, we'd take it."

Although Chumash on the reservation experienced poverty—after all, unlike everyone else in the adjacent town of Santa Ynez, they had no potable water, nor sewer, electric, or gas lines—many also have fond memories of that time.

> I have nothing but good memories of being raised on the Rez, because when you have family, you have birthdays, occasions, excellent food, a lot of food, everything freshly made, and then we would have our own musicians, a guitar player, a violinist, whatever. And, yeah, there was drinking. The women would start singing. I have real fond memories, even though it would end up"—and here Tonie laughs and puts up her fists,

indicating a fight—"at the end of the party. I still remember my grandma cooking cow heads. The ranchers would give her the head 'cause they knew she liked it.

She also has fond memories of her uncle Chicho and Joe Miranda growing vegetables and sharing them with others on the reservation, "fantastic crops, corn as sweet as sugar, tomatoes big and plump."

But although Tonie felt well protected and taken care of at home by her hardworking parents, she also had a keen awareness of the reservation residents being marginalized by the larger community.

Just because I walked from the Rez to the high school, the kids knew that 'Tonie's Indian,' and in a way I used to be ashamed 'cause we lived in a forty-five-foot trailer and all these kids were rich. They had a really good life, and I didn't have electricity, light, or water. So, my self-esteem went down. At that time, I really did not want to be identified as an Indian. Through my teenage life, I was ashamed. And it bothers me now that I am older. Why would I ever be ashamed of being part of the reservation? But this was the 1960s, when blacks were really being treated bad, and I didn't think that anyone with light skin would be treated bad in the valley, but they did. It has to do with money. We didn't have that money. My mom was a domestic cleaner, my father worked on ranches, and I went to school, and on weekends I would clean right here at the Sanja Cota Motel. I was twelve years old when I started working.

Tonie has a distinct memory of her first day in high school, when she was walking with a girl who was a friend from middle school and a boy who was a doctor's son.

At one point my friend turned to me and said, "Tonie, we're in high school now. Things change. You've got to get new friends." That's when I started realizing that I was going to be put in a group. I couldn't be popular with them 'cause they didn't want me to be around them. They knew I lived on the Rez. She just didn't want to be seen with me—that really hurt.

These conditions and social marginalization continued well into the '70s and '80s. The reservation was known as a fairly lawless place, with a high rate of alcoholism and drug abuse, and with many residents on welfare. Kathy Marshall, a language apprentice who has been active with education, says, "We were out there in line getting our government cheese and people were driving by, seeing us, because they used to do it right at the tribal hall. They'd pull up in their big semis and we would stand in line, and you know Highway 246 is just right there, and so, it was on display. So, yeah, they didn't want their family to be associated with us." Echoing Tonie's experiences from twenty-five years earlier, she says, "My brother had a girlfriend who was white and he went to meet her parents. And then she wasn't ever allowed to see him again because he was from the reservation."

But even some Chumash families avoided living on the reservation because of its associated problems. As one Chumash descendant in his late forties put it,

> We didn't live on the Rez because my mother didn't want us to live with the poverty, the welfare, alcohol, and all. You know, sometimes it takes generations to get out of poverty when you've been in it for generations. None of those people were ever working a good full-time job. A lot of them were gardeners and ranch hands and housekeepers; they were making minimum wage.

Marginalization in the wider community had negative effects on education and identity. The lack of education for Chumash in the mid-twentieth century comes through in all my interviews. Although Tonie graduated from Santa Ynez High School, her mother had gone to school only until she was thirteen years old. At one point there was a school on the reservation, but the teacher left because, according to Tonie, "he felt it was a waste. My mother was raised, 'You have to make money to live.' A lot of them didn't know how to read or write. You've got to work to put clothes on your back and food on the table; school wasn't important."

In addition to the lack of education, the cultural and linguistic suppression over the previous century had also left a lasting mark on indigenous identity, of which there was little at that point. Talking about her parents' generation, Tonie states,

They didn't know much about their life as Indians because the reservation was so poor, and I mean *poor*! I don't think that the Rez at the time was something to be proud of because they were so busy trying to make that dollar to feed the family and put clothes on your back. And I think the culture was so wiped out by the missions and the Spaniards and the Mexicans. But because of the depression caused by being so dirt poor, the culture wasn't really a big issue back then. My mother raised me to work and never really spoke of the culture and being an Indian. Back then, in the early '60s, I really think that we had been so suppressed that we ended up being ashamed of who we are. I was wearing makeup so heavy I looked like a *chola*, backcombing my hair so high and hiding behind my makeup. Why? Because I didn't think much of myself, because they looked down on the Rez—we were the slum of the '60s. You go to the city, you can see where the slum is at, but here it's a beautiful valley—and guess what? There's an Indian reservation there with no water, no lights, no gas!

But perhaps the greatest indicator of the marginalization of the Chumash and their lack of power is the fact that some native women were sterilized. Adelina Alva-Padilla, the spiritual leader of the tribe, became emotional as she related, "A child has to grow up knowing, 'Okay, I am the product of a sterilized mother.' We weren't good enough. My mother, she was an Indian, she wasn't good enough to have more children! Her sister was sterilized at a very young age; she didn't even have one child." The sterilization of some Chumash women is corroborated by others. Chumash descendant Freddy Romero, stocky, late forties, with a graying ponytail, tells me, "To kill off future generations they went around sterilizing them. I have two aunts who were sterilized for the sake of keeping them from having children. My uncle was able to help my mom escape that by hiding her so she was never sterilized." Indeed, according to Dominica Valencia, who was one generation removed from sterilization efforts, many elders in her parents' generation avoided clinics altogether out of fear of sterilization.

It is instructive to hear the testimonies of Chumash who didn't grow up on the reservation and their relationship to the community; they, too, were discriminated against because of their Indianness and had to suppress their culture. Dolores Cross and her sister Maxine Littlejohn grew up off the reservation. Like many other Chumash, they are part Filipino and grew up in the Five Cities area, specifically in Guadalupe and Arroyo Grande. Today, Dolores is on the Elders Committee. She now lives in the area called the "upper reservation" with a nice view of the Santa Ynez Mountains. We decided to go to their mother's house a block away for our interview. There I met their mother, Esther Manguray, born in the 1920s. Esther was in her mid-eighties and her daughters were in their fifties when interviewed.

Although their father was Filipino and their mother is Chumash and speaks Spanish and English, all those cultures got suppressed in their upbringing. They grew up on a ranch ten miles outside of Arroyo Grande, where their father was a farm worker. Dolores says, "My dad spoke his language, but he did not teach his language to us; my mom spoke Spanish, but we didn't speak that either. We just spoke English in our home. We didn't identify ourselves as Indian, even though my grandmother totally looked Indian. She lived on the reservation; we came to visit her here all the time. My dad did a lot of work at her house; he helped build it. So we were here all the time." Maxine relates that when she was growing up, "My mom said, 'Don't tell anyone you're Indian,' and that was just passed on to us. Saying you were Indian was taboo. You say you're Filipino. You know when you fill out all the forms in school? Ethnicity? Well, it wasn't a good idea to put Native American, and there was no space for Native American anyway!" "Native American" was, and still is, according to Dolores, synonymous with "poor, uneducated. That's the stereotype, even today the kids feel there's some prejudice."

But things were much worse in her mother's generation during the 1940s and '50s. Indeed, Dolores Cross says, nodding over at her mother, "When they were going to school, they segregated them. She went to the Sherman Indian School." Esther, who grew up on the reservation, confirms that fact; she was one of the few who went there voluntarily. Shaking her head, she states, "They took quite a few of us up there, all native from all over. They treated us pretty good, though we didn't really learn anything about native culture. We were supposed to work—we each had a job. I worked in the hospital, and I worked in the kitchen and the post office."

Esther and several other Chumash were some of the hundreds of American Indian children removed from their homes and communities to be taught a trade and to be educated in a way that would have them conform

48

to Euro-American society. Niki Sandoval, a Chumash descendant and current education director for the tribe, who interviewed Santa Ynez Chumash elders in her 2007 study of educational politics, found that native students at the Sherman Institute were lonely and that the administrators fostered mistrust between Chumash and other native groups. The native students "spent most of the day engaged in vocational curriculum that focused on domestic work." Later, when Esther looked for work, she found her education there did not help. "When you looked for a job and said you were from Sherman Institute, they didn't hire you," she says laughing. "They'd think something's wrong with you, as if you had been institutionalized."

Esther continued to be treated differently from her neighbors in the valley, even after having been uprooted from her family and community. Esther returned to the reservation, but when she met her husband-to-be, a Filipino, she was not allowed to marry him in California. She had to go to Arizona to get a marriage license. "Mixed marriages" were illegal in the Golden State.

Cultural Revitalization in the 1960s

One has to be careful when characterizing the revitalization of Indian identity that began in the late 1960s and the culture loss that preceded it. Many of my interviews with Chumash elders and descendants indicate that in Santa Ynez, the Chumash language and culture had been almost completely lost by the late '60s. Although some elders still knew some of the language, the last fluent speaker of the language had already died by then. Songs, prayers, ceremony, and traditional knowledge were passed down in a few families, but it was fragmented at best. Most of what began to be recovered in the late '60s was taken from the anthropological and historical literature about the Chumash, and this work served as the basis for cultural reinvention.

Language is one window into culture loss and retrieval. Richard Applegate, linguist and former director of the Chumash Language Program, was hired by the tribe to help bring back the language. As a doctoral student, he reconstructed the Samala (or Ineseño) language in the late '60s entirely from the notes taken by J.P. Harrington in the early twentieth century. In the '60s, there were only "a few words still in current use.... It might be like third-generation Jews who know a few words of Yiddish that they use in their conversation."

Some Chumash, however, say that some elder women sang songs and spoke Chumash to each other behind closed doors until their deaths in the 1970s and '80s. For example, Esther, who was born in the 1920s, remembers her mother—who died at ninety years of age in 1985—speaking the language, although she refused to teach it to her children; indeed, she did not even want them listening in. Tonie Flores says that her mother and grandmother would not teach her the dances, songs, or stories. Other relatives in her grandparents' generation "knew some Chumash but they weren't allowed to speak it. Their parents weren't allowed to speak it. They were not allowed to speak Chumash because they remembered the past. 'Don't you dare talk Chumash or else you'll get in trouble.' Our culture was pretty much destroyed, and Indians had to secretly speak their language or they'd get in trouble. And that's the truth."

Some Chumash tell me that despite the intense cultural pressures to abandon any identification with things Indian, some indigenous culture, though fragmented, continued on in the '50s, including "sweats" (purification through sweat lodges), songs, wearing of regalia, and ceremony. But others stress that by that time—after two centuries of cultural suppression and the last half of that "passing" as Mexicans for survival—there was little left for the cultural revivalists of the '60s to build on. Rather, they had to use the anthropological and historical record to revitalize the culture.

A strong wave of cultural revitalization began in the late '60s and early '70s with the work of Anthony Romero and Pete Crowheart Zavalla, who were influenced by the burgeoning civil rights movement, including the American Indian Movement (AIM), found across the country. Tonie states, "Pete and Tony Romero got along so well. And all of a sudden they started drumming and dancing together. It was natural. They enjoyed what they were doing, and pretty soon people started asking them to dance at schools, at functions, parades, museums, grade schools. They went all over Santa Barbara County, up north, down south, anywhere there was a pow wow." Although Zavalla and Romero were not the only traditionalists, they did have a large impact. Pow wows began to be held on the reservation, partly to raise money for different projects such as getting potable water to the reservation and partly because of the growing pow wow circuit in the '70s. According to Pete Zavalla, Campbell Grant's book on cave paintings gave them the initial impetus to push forward their cultural projects.

Desi Zavalla, Santa Ynez Chumash, at a pow wow in the 1970s. His father, Pete Zavalla, was a key figure in the revitalization movement of those years. Photo courtesy of Tonie Flores.

They had a significant impact on the lives of many young Chumash. Kathy Marshall remembers that when she was a girl, one of the cultural revitalists "would pick us up in his El Camino, and we'd just all pack into the back and he'd take us to the old tribal hall. We would get some granite rocks and we would paint rock art. He would teach us songs in our language. We never really made any regalia because it was expensive; I remember some kids having regalia but that's just 'cause their parents went out and got it for them. Our classes were what he could afford; you know, it came from him, his words and his songs."

The net effect of the cultural movements of the late 1960s, Tonie tells me, was that it "became okay to be Indian. We didn't care what people thought; we did what we had to do, and it was just natural. Everything that has been happening has been getting stronger and stronger, instead of weaker, because now the pride is there. Way back then the prejudice was so heavy."

Within the non-Chumash community, there was a backlash to this assertion of native identity. Although the "folkloric" display of Chumash culture was tolerated and even celebrated by some of the non-Indian locals, other events of those days point to conflict. For example, in the high school, one Chumash boy who grew his hair long and wore the red bandana of the emerging Indian rights movement was sent home from school. As one Chumash woman told me, "The high school told him, 'Don't come back unless you cut your hair!' Well, he talked to his family, and Pete Zavalla got involved and they ended up calling AIM, and they came down to help the cause. And the school didn't know what to do. 'Who is this group?' And the boy was allowed back in school."

Dominica Valencia gives me another example of discrimination when the Indian boys and men started growing their hair long. "I remember one time, they used to have a bar called 'The First and Last Chance' in Santa Ynez. And I was sitting there, and all of a sudden these two cowboys came out of a bar. And this Indian guy, he was walking into the bar and they said, 'Hey Indian, where's your blanket?' and he turned around and told him, 'Yeah, I left it with your wife.' Well, they got in a fight," she says, laughing. "That kind of thing would happen often."

Nevertheless, conditions began to change for the better in the late 1960s and early 1970s. Dominica tells me, "In the sixties, with the cultural revolution, the hippie era, things were changing. Vietnam was happening, so there was a whole different direction back then." In 1967, several barbecues and "pow wows" for the general public and other fundraisers were put on by the "improvement committee" of the eleven extended families living on the reservation. A local "Concerned Citizens" group was also formed to help the tribe.

As a result, economic conditions for the Chumash started to improve. The reservation finally got potable water, electricity, gas, and a sewer system. Some individuals returned to the reservation in the late 1970s when Housing and Urban Development (HUD) began to build government-subsidized houses; a minor housing boom on the reservation began, and people began perceiving some benefits from being Indian. Health issues on the reservation—the high incidence of alcoholism, diabetes, and other problems—also began to be addressed around this time, when Rosa Pace established a small clinic in a trailer. Although it had an important impact on the tribe, it was a modest operation consisting of one doctor, a nurse, and an assistant in a double-wide trailer. In class terms, the Chumash continued to share a lot in common with the working-class Mexican population, with whom they were often confused.

The appearance of the bingo parlor in the mid-1980s began to generate some employment and benefits, and more people returned to live on the reservation. More economic opportunities opened up when, in 1994, the Chumash began offering slot-machine games, and, with tribal people working the floor and providing security, the profits began to pour in. By December 2001, when the tribe held three days of festivities to celebrate one hundred years as a federally recognized tribe, they could afford nationally recognized musicians and comedians. A tented structure served as the casino until the new casino and resort was built in 2003 with the tribe investing $157 million. More important for our purposes here, the tribe also built a new Tribal Hall and health clinic on the west side of the casino in 2002. A center for many cultural and educational activities, the Tribal Hall is a beautiful building; with the large Chumash flag billowing over it, it is a vital symbol of how far the tribe has come. Indeed, for the Chumash themselves, the Tribal Hall, not the casino, is the focal point of their community.

The Chumash Casino. The casino revenues have allowed the Chumash to reverse a long history of educational, economic, political, and cultural marginalization. Photo by Gary Robinson.

The Santa Ynez Chumash Today

The Santa Ynez Band of Chumash Indians is one of several groups of Chumash, who, as a whole, number more than five thousand individuals. As mentioned before, the Santa Ynez group is the only one that is federally recognized, and is one of more than a hundred such recognized tribes in California. Although very much connected through marriage, culture, and social activities with the rest of the valley populace, the Chumash are also very much a separate people with a distinct culture and heritage.

Today, while many Chumash live off-reservation, "approximately three hundred people reside on the reservation, which is located on 126 acres." Among the Santa Ynez Band, there are both tribal "members" and "descendants," two different categories. The former, who number around one hundred and fifty individuals, have "¼ blood" and have been approved by an Enrollment Committee. Members receive monthly per capita payouts. But these hundred and fifty or so members have over twelve hundred descendants, and these individuals benefit directly from the casino revenues. These benefits include education funds for all levels, as discussed in chapter five.

How can we characterize this population today? As far as their physical appearance, most Chumash are brown-skinned with stereotypically "Indian" or "Mexican" features. But others do not have these, because of intermarriage with European Americans, Filipinos, and African-Americans. Tribal members and their descendants come in all colors, from white to black and every shade in between. Culturally, a hybrid culture emerged among the Santa Ynez Chumash, one that draws on Spanish, Indian, and Mexican life ways and often combines them with mainstream American culture and social forms.

Of course, this idea of Chumash culture is at odds with the usually static, diorama-like representations that prevail at present. We have to look at their lived experience today. Chumash culture is not just material artifacts such as woven baskets and rock art, but rather is something based on a shared historical experience and identity, one that is increasingly being recognized and assimilated by descendants.

In characterizing the Chumash today, one must address the negative and misdirected stereotypes used by the dominant society. One of these is that the Chumash are inauthentic. This view assumes that Indians should be "pure" and ignores the colonial processes by which they were disenfranchised, economically, culturally, and politically. For example, many times during my years in the area, I have heard people say things such as, "Well, you know, they aren't even really Indian; they've all got Mexican last names." Such a view ignores the fact that most indigenous people in other parts of the former Spanish colonies, especially Mexico, also have Spanish surnames. The Chumash have to be understood within the history of Indian and Spanish and Mexican miscegenation, that is, biological mixing, and of the larger history of Latin America, of which the Chumash were once part.

The mixture with the Spanish-speaking world is complex. Many Chumash speak Spanish and are married to Mexicans—often people, like them, of mixed Spanish/Indian descent. But nevertheless, when Chumash speak Spanish it is often accented. Some only understand but don't speak the language. So, too, their spoken English is often markedly different from that of other residents in the valley; it has a different cadence, apparently influenced by long-standing speaking patterns based partly on American Indian and Spanish syntax and grammar, as well as local ranch culture.

In addition to linguistic differences from the Mexican and white residents of the valley, a set of orientations and cultural practices differentiates them, such as a different kind of respect for elders and a different orientation to ancestors, ceremony, and sweats. Knowledge of a shared history and culture found in stories, songs, dance, regalia, ceremony, and protocol increasingly defines Santa Ynez Chumash collective identity in opposition to the identities of other people in the valley.

Much cultural performance, however, takes place outside the public purview. Although the public is invited to look over the shoulders of the Chumash, so to speak, at the Annual Chumash Intertribal Pow Wow and the annual Tomol Crossing, many celebrations and rituals put on by the tribe today (such as the Bear Ceremony, the Maria Solares Celebration, and the Ramada Gathering) are for Chumash only. These and other cultural reclamation projects have further strengthened Chumash ritual, culture, and historical knowledge about the tribe.

Another feature in Chumash group identity is a historical consciousness of being oppressed and suppressed, of cultural loss, of the reservation having long been a different social space in the valley, and a shared sense of having been marginalized by the larger community. This sentiment and knowledge of shared history also join the Chumash to a larger group of American Indians, as do certain features of Native North American culture in general, which get strong reinforcement during the annual pow wows and other intertribal gatherings. However, I do not want to give the impression of dour, victimized Indians. The Chumash I know have a great sense of humor, among other things, using playful irony when dealing with dominant stereotypes about Indians.

In addition to strengthening the tribal government and collective identity and power of the tribe, the casino revenues have wiped out most of the poverty on the reservation. Construction has been booming, and the reservation now has its own health clinic, fire department, and education department. The reservation or "the Rez" has a unique feel to it today, no longer the "Indian ghetto" or "slum of the valley," as some described it in the past. Today the trailers and prefab houses, with an occasional custom-made home, clustered together on relatively small lots in the upper reservation, offer a strong contrast with the large landholdings and lawn-fronted homes of much of the valley.

Because residences are built close together, the reservation has the feel of a close-knit village—that is, of people, mostly interrelated, living in close proximity. With extended families living side by side and the sounds of playing children and bikes and motorcycles running around the neighborhoods, there is a density of social relations not found in the larger population. At the same time, many Chumash live off-reservation, many in nice residences and small ranches in the valley or in nearby Lompoc or Los Alamos. Other Chumash live further afield, visiting the reservation only occasionally.

The Chumash and their descendants are not the only economic beneficiaries of the casino. The second-largest employer in Santa Barbara County (the first being the county itself), the tribe controls not only the casino, restaurants, entertainment showroom, and resort associated with its main enterprise, but several other business ventures in the area. The Chumash flag, alongside the Californian and American flags, is seen today flying over the casino-resort, the Tribal Hall and Health Clinic and also over a gas station, the former Royal Scandinavian Hotel in Solvang, and other commercial properties. The tribe has also been trying to develop other properties, such as 6.9 acres for a Tribal Museum and Cultural Center, and the recently purchased fourteen hundred acres of pristine valley land. The tribe has attempted to put these lands into trust, basically annexing them to the reservation, and this has met with fierce opposition from the tribe's local opponents.

Tribal Hall and Tribal Health Clinic. While the Tribal Hall is at the center of Chumash self-government and a source of pride for the Chumash community, the Tribal Health Clinic provides health care to the low income residents of the valley of all ethnicities. Photo by Gary Robinson.

Some of the opposition voices are reasonable, voicing concern over the general direction that development in the valley is taking. But, as detailed in subsequent chapters, others are less so, spreading misinformation about the tribe and making extremely personal attacks on the Chumash and their heritage. These unreasonable critics claim that the Chumash already have enough, that they are turning the valley into a "company town," that they are not "real" Indians, and that their attempts to revitalize their culture and many contributions to the community are just cynical public relations maneuverings.

But, as we shall see, this is not the case, and the mark of the tribe's generosity is all over the valley. The tribe now has the economic wherewithal not only to support their own community but to help others less fortunate than themselves. One example is the new Tribal Clinic, a large, state-of-the-art medical facility with over thirty-five employees, which serves not just Chumash but the entire community, providing medical, dental, and mental health services. The only provider to accept Medical in the valley, the clinic serves people from every income level, including the valley's poorest. It takes care of the predominantly Latino workforce of domestics, gardeners, and farm workers, as well as white service industry workers. In so doing, it helps to subsidize the households, ranches, vineyards, and businesses that employ these individuals. In addition to assuring that the Chumash themselves obtain the health services they need, the clinic is a major benefit to the whole valley.

The tribe has also established the Santa Ynez Band of Chumash Indians Foundation, which has donated over $16 million over the past years. The tribe also hosts many fundraisers for organizations that serve the needy. The beneficiaries of these fundraisers and the foundation include the local hospital, high school, YMCA, many local non-profit organizations, and numerous causes. The tribe takes pride in this, especially when it helps an organization that, before the casino, supported tribal members in harder times.

***

In sum, the tribe has come a long way in the last century. From a history of marginalization, poverty, and cultural suppression, the tribe is now a major economic engine for the whole region. With the purchase of the Royal Scandinavian Inn (today Hotel Corque), it became the largest taxpayer in the city of Solvang. The casino resort and its entertainment venues bring considerable entertainment and tourism to the region. With its charitable foundation and health clinic, the tribe gives back considerably to the community.

In this and the previous chapter, we have seen the historical forces allied against the tribe and how the Chumash have lifted themselves out of poverty and powerlessness to attain great wealth and political and economic strength. These historical materials provide the necessary context for understanding the particular processes surrounding education and culture discussed in part two. They also frame our discussion of the cultural politics in the valley today, which is the subject of the next chapter.

ANACAPA
SANTA ROSA
SANTA CRUZ
SANTA BARBARA CHA
Santa Barbara
SAN MARCOS PASS
SANTA YNE
MOUN
154
PARADISE ROAD
KALAWASHAQ
lake Cachuma
CHUMASH RESERVATION
TRIBAL HALL
CLINIC
CASINO
santa ynez river
246
HAPPY CANYON ROAD
Santa Ynez
Santa Ynez High School
THE CHUMASH HIGHWAY
REFUGIO ROAD
Ballard
ALAMO PINTADO ROAD
S
E
W
N
154
Los Olivos
MATTEI'S TAVERN
FIGUEROA
MTN.
FIGUEROA MTN. ROAD
SOXT
SAN RAF
EMMA MUNGER 2012

Three

Current Cultural Politics in the Valley

"A dominant society often projects onto minority 'others' its collective fears and concerns. The general sense among many people living in the United States today is that the capitalist-driven pace of living is too fast, that we are consumed by materialist values, and that notions of community and family are being compromised in the process. In short, projecting onto Native Americans a 'backward' and 'non-modern' lifestyle is vital to help non-Indians feel better about themselves and their future in a turbulent and fast-changing world. The price of this projection, however, is that it helps sustain false ideas about Native peoples and locks into place shallow stereotypes and cultural understandings about them that provide the breeding ground for intolerance, stigmatization, and discrimination."

Eve Darian-Smith, legal anthropologist

In the previous chapters, we saw that people of Chumash descent, despite population decline and cultural loss, were still a significant percentage of the small valley population at the end of the nineteenth century. With the establishment of white settlers and towns, the Chumash became even more marginalized socially, economically, politically, and culturally than before. But we also saw that the tribe

62

overcame tremendous adversity and that it has moved from poverty to great prosperity.

Nevertheless, that the tribe has had an antagonistic relationship with the community in which it has been embedded would be hard to deny. This relationship extends to the present. Part of this has to do with cultural politics and the region's "heritage," the way that history is remembered and particular cultures publicly celebrated. Which cultures get represented and valued, and which do not? On the whole, it is white culture—that of the Spanish Vaqueros, the Western ranching traditions, and the Danish culture of Solvang—that is considered the valley's heritage, and it is celebrated in town festivals, museums, the education system, and local publications.

Diversity beneath the Surface

If you were to glean an impression of the valley from the tourist magazines and most local publications, you would conclude that its population is homogenous: upper-middle class, white, and privileged. Wineries, ranches, fine restaurants, fleets of luxury cars, as well as golfing and biking, mark the area as upscale and generally white. Contrary to the image projected through these media and most local celebrations, far more economic, social, and cultural diversity exists beneath the surface.

The valley has been multicultural for a long time. Before the Spanish invasion, the Chumash themselves engaged other cultures and social groups through trade, rituals, and intermarriage. Chumash and Spanish were spoken in the valley long before English and Danish, and over the last century and a half, people from China, the Philippines, and Mexico migrated there. There is also great diversity within the Latino community residing in the valley. Some Mexican families have longstanding roots in the valley stretching back many generations. Others have only been here a generation or two, and still others have recently arrived to work in the fields and service sector. Many of the people planting crops along the main thoroughfares of the valley speak as their first language not Spanish but Mixtec or Zapotec, indigenous languages from the south of Mexico. In fact, many nonwhite peoples in addition to the Chumash have had a social presence in the valley but rarely get mentioned—and certainly not valued or celebrated—in local media and ritual celebrations.

Although there is a kind of de facto segregation between the wealthy and predominantly white land-owning class and the brown Latino working class (who mow their lawns, work their ranches and vineyards, clean their houses, and work in the service sector), there is also much greater economic diversity than generally meets the eye in the valley, and this diversity crosses all ethnic groups. Although Mexican culture often gets associated with the poor farm workers and service sector workers, in fact there are many wealthy Latinos in the valley as well as a strong and growing Latino middle class. There are also poor whites in the valley, many of whom work in the service sector. And there are many white-collar workers there who commute to Santa Barbara. With the generally upscale nature of valley life and the median price for a house above four hundred thousand dollars, many blue-collar and white-collar workers now commute from Lompoc or Santa Maria to work in the valley. Some valley residents live in mansions, some live in tract homes, and some live in dingy trailers. Some bike to lose weight and some bike to get to work.

White Heritage and Exclusion

They say that history is written by the victors. This is certainly the case for the valley, where local histories, the educational system, and the ritual calendar all remember and celebrate the area's white heritage. The history of the valley is presented in the local popular media and rituals as basically white, going back to the Spanish colonial period (the Fiesta Celebration and the recent two hundredth anniversary celebration of Mission Santa Ynez) and its relatively white hacienda culture (with the Chumash reduced to folkloric caricatures), the Western lifestyle of ranchers that developed after California statehood, and the Danish influence in Solvang. Although local Mexicans and other Latinos do have the annual one-day Fiesta Celebration at Mission Santa Ynez in Solvang, it ostensibly—like the Fiesta of Santa Barbara ("Old Spanish Days")—celebrates the Spanish, not Mexican, culture associated with the missions. On the whole, the festival calendar commemorates Western and Danish heritage through Solvang's Danish Days and the Western-themed Santa Ynez Day, Los Olivos Day, and Los Alamos Day. It is this heritage and the emerging wine culture (now celebrated in wine festivals) that really have center stage in the local presentation of self.

Exclusion, whether through ritual celebration or outright racism and overt prejudice, finds many forms in the valley. While some local ranchers, farmers, and vintners are progressive, others have a retrograde view of Latinos and immigrant workers. Although they often depend on illegal Latino immigrant labor for their enterprises, they rail against illegal immigration in local newspapers and public presentations. They would deny basic services, like health and education, to the very people on whose backs they have built up their enterprises. Many Latinos in the valley have suffered the barbs and stings of racist comments and behavior in institutional settings such as schools (where they are sometimes treated as naturally inferior students with no capacity for higher education), and in everyday interactions in stores and on the street. The same is true of the Chumash.

Things have gotten much better over the years, and I do not want to paint a picture of total exclusion. Today, there are many positive interactions among Latinos, Chumash, and white residents through familial ties, friendships, and cross-cultural activities. Many of the ranchers, farmers, and vintners appreciate and honor their Latino workers; several of the prominent winemakers of the area are even of Mexican descent. Deep ties between white owners and Latino workers often go well beyond the social contract and into abiding trust and friendship.

It used to be much worse for both Latinos and Chumash. Indeed, in talking with the Chumash, one gets a strong sense not only of how they were confused with Mexicans but of how both groups were routinely treated as inferior beings. As a third-generation white man who is sympathetic to the Chumash told me,

> I grew up with it and saw it, and it was just horrible what the Chumash went through. I can tell you stories. Some of the local rednecks would be cruising in their trucks and when they saw an Indian riding their bike, they'd knock them off with a broomstick—awful stuff. For many of them the Reservation was a place to go carousing or fighting after they'd been drinking.

Today, the fact that the tribe has gone from being economically incorporated in a negative way in the valley (as a "slum" without services and dependent on welfare) to being a major economic powerhouse with political clout and wealthy members has led to new forms of prejudice and exclusion. As Frances Snyder, a tribal member and former Chumash spokesperson, told me,

> The tribal opponents are all about being against the tribe, even though they continually say it's about the *process* or about *circumventing the rules*, or about *tribal government*. The bottom line is that it's all about the tribal people. They liked us much better when tribal members were their housekeepers, ranch hands, and gardeners. Now that some tribal members drive luxury cars like them, they hate it. We have upset the apple cart and moved past the station in life that they had assigned to us—and it kills them.

When I asked her whether the situation has improved for the Chumash kids of this generation, Frances told me, "Nothing has changed. It has always been bad, and it will always be bad. The racist kids who threw rocks at my mother taught their children to be just as nasty. And, what's worse, some of the very wealthy so-called celebrities have come into the area and brought with them a nasty, elitist attitude." Other Chumash feel the same way. In her eighties, Esther Manguray says that the Chumash are not liked, and she feels it every day. "We just ignore them. It does not seem to them that we could have something nice, like we can't have a nice car. You drive your car and it's the way they look at you—they just give you a dirty look. Why? I don't know. They're prejudiced."

Stereotypes of the Chumash

Stereotypes of the Chumash, and current debates about the tribe and its casino, have to be understood within stereotypes of American Indians in general. Indigenous people throughout the Americas are often treated as "noble savages" or as just plain "savage." When they are seen as savages, the underlying assumption is racist: it views Indians as naturally inferior, as destined to die out or occupy a lower order, as unable to cope with modern industrial society. "The implicit message is: If 'they' were equal to 'us,' so many of them wouldn't still be living in squalid poverty," and if they are getting ahead, it is only because they are given an unfair advantage. In this view, Indians are "lawless" and "do not pay taxes" nor do they have the capacity to manage a business and are just dupes for predatory Las Vegas types.

The other stereotype, that of the "noble savage," is even more insidious. As scholar Eve Darian-Smith points out, an argument that surfaces again and again in opposition to Chumash economic expansion is that

> if Native Americans really loved the land and had a spiritual affinity with nature, as they supposedly do, then how could they possibly be advocating for a large building development on their own reservation? This argument harks back to a romanticized stereotype of Native Americans as being, in effect, remnants of a prehistoric age—spiritual, communal, untouched and unblemished by the corruption of modern society.

As one public official said a few years back, "They have, you know, taken up a really beautiful legacy of basketry and tommel (sic) building, and really interesting lifestyles and sort of erased it with one fell swoop."

This stereotype reveals an amazing ignorance of the Chumash's previous poverty and the ways that Chumash culture has been beaten down by the dominant society over generations; it also gives the impression of an ahistorical people, static in time and removed from the rest of the world. As Darian-Smith puts it,

> [T]he historical image of Native American peoples is that they live quite literally in another world, untouched and unblemished by capitalist morals, deeply connected to land and nature, and upholding family and community relationships as central to their communal lifestyle. Native Americans often represent an idealized and romanticized vision of a past era, and a model of social relations no longer available or accessible to a majority of people.

A prime example of this mentality is found in a 2004 paid advertisement in a local newspaper. Written by a famous songwriter and endorsed by other famous musicians and actors who live in the valley, the ad attacked the development plans of the Chumash and the tribal chairman himself. "I find it ironic that a man who claims to be part of a culture whose ideology is founded on the principle of preserving the land is so dead set on defiling it." He goes on to quote Crazy Horse ("One does not sell the earth the people walk upon") before stating, "I can only imagine how the burial grounds of his ancestors must be convulsing with pain at the thought of such treachery."

So, these are the choices, according to these two views: either Indians are a baser and lower type of humanity, unable to be part of modern society and run businesses, or they are pure of heart and close to the land. If natives get rich, they lose traditional culture. "The underlying assumption of these attitudes is that Indian peoples are only truly Indian if they are poor, out of sight and out of mind on faraway reservations, and are not part of mainstream society." In sum, "good Indians" worship the earth; "bad Indians" make money. Why, asks Darian-Smith, should Indians be subjected to a different moral code? And how, I would add, can critics of the Chumash be so willfully ignorant of the sad history of their neighbors and what the valley's development over the last centuries has meant for them?

Support for the Chumash

While their voice is not as loud and shrill as that of the Chumash's opponents, many people in the valley back the tribe. This is expressed in local forums, in letters to the editor, and op-ed pieces in local publications. Many residents think that Indians have been oppressed for too long and deserve to get ahead, and that special rights are necessary to level the playing field. One local man in his thirties who has ties in the valley stretching back several generations says he knows what the Chumash went through and that he differs from a lot of his friends in his regard for them. "I say, hey, this valley used to be all theirs. I say let them get all they can. They deserve it." And a third-generation resident of the valley, a soft-spoken and thoughtful man in his fifties, commented to me, "The people who have been here for a while, who've seen how the Chumash were treated, aren't the ones making all the fuss. It's these newbies who came up from LA, sometimes land developers themselves, and who've been around only for the last twenty years or so."

Many Chumash feel the same way. As one elder told me, "We know who all the old families are around here. It's these new people making the fuss." A descendant in his late forties, who has lived in the valley his whole life, says much the same. "I know a lot of the old timers who live here. The Concerned Citizens are all out-of-towners, they're definitely out-of-towners. There might be a few old ranchers in there, but it's always been names that I haven't recognized." He continues, "It's gotten to the point now that the valley is not the valley I grew up in. The people who are complaining and saying that they're locals, they're not locals. Fifteen years doesn't make you a local. And what really bothers me is that it filters down to the children. It affects the native children that go to school. It's just sad."

Clearly, the construction of the casino and the empowerment of the once-marginalized Chumash have upset traditional power arrangements and the local political order of the valley. We return to these issues in greater depth in the third and last part of the book. But now, let us turn to part two and to the considerable advances that the Chumash have made in education and cultural revitalization.

Part II

Culture and Education

Four

Education and Marginalization

"The only statewide curriculum standard that includes American Indians is in the fourth grade when public schools learn about early California history... The inclusion of Native peoples in the California curriculum standards stops in the mission period. This is a disservice to all students."

Chumash Education Director Niki Sandoval

The first part of this book used broad strokes to sketch the historical experience of the Chumash and the valley, and the effects of that experience on cultural politics today. We now go deeper into education and culture, which today are inseparable processes for the Chumash. They used to be at total odds, with education tied to cultural loss. Today, as detailed below, the tribe is overcoming that sad history. The native pride movements of the late 1960s and then the casino revenues ushered in a flurry of educational and cultural initiatives that have strengthened the tribe greatly. These initiatives now work together to assure that Chumash youth and older descendants learn both cultural pride and how to succeed in mainstream American society.

This second part of the book relies on Chumash narratives about their educational experiences and about those of their parents, grandparents, and children. It is important to hear the voices of the Chumash themselves, voices which often get erased by local history-making or muted by the contentions of their opponents.

1940s and '50s

Longstanding elements of educational segregation, prejudice, and open discrimination were still very much present in this region of California in the 1940s and '50s. Adelina Alva-Padilla, a Chumash traditionalist born in the 1930s who grew up "off-Rez" in the Arroyo Grande area to the north of the valley, remembers those times. With a resentful edge to her voice, she tells me, "We used to sit in the back of the bus; we Indians and the Mexicans were all mixed together and in the back. All the whites were in the front." She continues, "We weren't good enough to go into the seventh or eighth grade; we were put into the cafeteria. And then they wouldn't even teach us! I graduated from the eighth grade not knowing what four times four was!" When I ask her whether it was even tougher for little girls than for boys, Adelina replies with emphasis, "It was tougher for both of them if you were of color."

Chumash kids living on the reservation, as Niki Sandoval found in her study of educational politics there, have suffered bad treatment and exclusion for at least three generations. Several individuals who attended elementary school in the valley in the '50s distinctly remember the Indians and the Mexicans being grouped together and segregated from the whites during recess and lunch. While she documents some positive interactions, Sandoval's study provides many examples of behaviors ranging from subtle disrespect and rudeness to outright racism and the discrimination of Chumash youth by teachers, school administrators, and other parents at school and school events. The testimonies of individuals from the reservation that I gathered corroborate this and Sandoval's finding that the "low expectations and segregationist treatment of students in the local and regional schools are significant in their long lasting effects on students."

Until the 1960s, most Chumash didn't graduate from high school, let alone think about college. Esther Manguray, who is in her eighties, says that in her generation there were "none, absolutely none, going to college." Rather, many Chumash youth were not allowed to attend the high school and instead were shipped away to the Sherman Institute. As we saw in chapter two, this was an alienating experience, one in which "education" was diametrically opposed to culture.

Indeed, the assimilationist education provided by the missionaries that the Chumash received during the mission period and after continued through the 1940s at schools such as the Saint Boniface Indian School in Banning and the Sherman Institute, discussed earlier. At these schools, supported by the American government and the Catholic Church, students were punished for speaking their native language, their hair was cut, and children from different tribes were often thrust into an antagonistic relationship with each other. As Niki Sandoval tells me, "They were supposed to be learning reading, writing, and math, but according to the people that I have spoken to who actually went there in the forties, they spent maybe an hour on academic basics, very basic reading and writing and arithmetic. The rest of the day was spent cleaning and doing the laundry for the nuns; for the boys it was learning how to fix things, maintenance." They were basically training native people for the domestic service industry. Freddy Romero states, "People talk as if it were deep in the past. They're surprised when I talk about my mother and her sisters and brothers and how they were rounded up and taken from her parents. Some kids were beaten and sexually abused. The whole thing just angers me. I don't really like to hear about those stories."

In the '50s some Chumash graduated from grade school and a few from high school. Dominica Valencia says that in the '50s, her mom was lucky and the exception to the rule. "She had a high school education but as far as college or junior college at that time, it was not acceptable." Many Chumash of that generation never even learned how to read and write well. "Your education was maybe up to eighth grade, if you were lucky; that whole generation did not get a good education. You're talking about a generation that still put their money in a coffee can."

1960s to '90s

In the late 1960s, the cultural revitalization and Indian Pride movements on the reservation and in the general civil rights movement throughout the country had an impact on the educational system. Yet, exclusion and segregation, while taking different forms than before, continued.

It is important to emphasize that in the past there were, and today there are, a lot of positive interactions between diverse ethnic groups at

Santa Ynez Valley Union High School. That's why, before going into the antagonism and discrimination that many Chumash students have experienced, it is necessary to underline that many of them also felt included socially and liked many of their teachers. Some of them even managed to go on to higher education. Many Chumash who have gone to the high school are of mixed descent—white, Mexican, and Chumash—and some individuals can move easily among these different groups. There have been a lot of friendships, dating, and even marriages among these groups. Even those Chumash who suffered the worst at the high school also made strong friendships and bonds with local whites, friendships that last until this day.

Yet the discrimination experienced by many students worked against Chumash education and advancement. Some teachers prejudged Chumash youth, who were often assumed to be intellectually inferior and were put into the "continuation" school on campus—ostensibly developed "to serve students with behavioral, learning, and physical differences who were not well served in mainstream classrooms"—or "special ed," and they were never "tracked" for college but rather for menial jobs. The Chumash themselves were absent in the curriculum, and the educational system continued to militate against Chumash cultural identity or cultural pride.

As Dominica Valencia tells me, in the early '70s,

> [T]here were a lot of immigrants. We had a lot of farm workers; so we had different social groups. We had the kids that were, of course, wealthy and white, and then we had the Mexican kids that had their own group. At that time, we were called 'Chicanos,' 'wetbacks,' 'beaners' because the natives mostly hung around with the Mexicans because we just figured we were the same. We didn't want to be pointed out, 'Oh, there's the Indians over there,' so we kept to ourselves and we inter-grouped with the Mexican people.

There was no distinct Chumash group in the high school at that time, she says.

Kathy Marshall, who went to the high school in the late '80s, says,

> It was mixed for me. I never really felt like I fit in. Before we moved to the reservation we lived in Solvang. I went to Solvang

elementary school. There were only myself and a couple of other kids of color in the school, so I never felt comfortable. But when I got to the high school we all sort of joined together, but you know there was a separation for sure. I know that it is still there today. But just in my own personal experience I had some friends that were white in elementary school, and so when I got to high school I had already established my own little friendships with them. So I think I was in between. All the Rez kids hung out together, so I was able to cross through and have both sides, and with Latinos, too. My dad's Hispanic so I had my cousins there as well. So I was able to jump around a little bit. But the Rez kids were the Rez kids, the Hispanics were the Hispanics. They were definitely separated. There were the aggies, the cowboys, you had the stoners and then you had the jocks, pretty much what every high school has. The Hispanics were definitely separated, and the natives were separated. I remember people calling names back and forth, but I don't recall any huge rivalry. But of course I was in the middle.

Willie Wyatt, who is Chumash, white, and Mexican, had a similar experience. "I kind of fit in with any group, was seen just as everybody else. Other kids from the reservation had a harder time fitting in. There was some tension and some fighting growing up. I think my experience was different because I fit in." He tells me the valley was different back then and that his experience at the high school was positive for the most part. "There was our group from the reservation. We had a lot of friends. We were just another part of the social scene at the high school, and when we had high school parties (occasionally there were some of those on the reservation), but there was no us and them. We had friends from different ethnic groups. There were social cliques—the jocks, the aggies, the stoners, the drama types—but everyone kind of mixed. There *was* a separation between the college-bound students and the social-scene people."

Some ethnicities and cultures were more highly valued than others. Willie says,

I think there was a little bit of that bigoted attitude in the Santa Ynez Valley in general because it's not very culturally diverse. There aren't a lot of black families in the Santa Ynez Valley—one or two African-American families, your Caucasian group, and the migrant farm worker group, and then the reservation. There was really only three cultures represented; the Asian population was and is still a minority. So, I think there was some tension there, a bigoted attitude that kind of rubs off on everybody. I caught myself kind of having a bad attitude, and as I got older and matured, I kind of wondered where that came from.

Carmen Sandoval, who graduated from the high school in 1990, remembers wondering where she fit in her freshman year. There were

the rich kids, the drama people, music and band kids, all these little cliques, the aggies, the jocks, the stoners, and the Hispanics. I was immediately drawn to the Hispanic community. I don't know if it was because they were a minority as well, but I was able to speak a little bit of Spanish as my dad is from Mexico (my parents divorced when I was six and he didn't live with us), and my mother spoke fluent Spanish for work. So in high school, I drifted to the Hispanics, but I thought, *I am not Hispanic*. Then we had the Rez crew, but I never really found myself in just one group but had friends in many groups. In high school I felt discrimination from the teachers mostly, but there were a few that were really cool and who I really adored, really wonderful teachers. But the bad ones would single you out in class. If a rich kid was talking then he would have no punishment; things would just kind of move along. But if a Rez kid would be talking out of turn or something, they'd have to be held after class or shown the right way because apparently they didn't know it. It was very obvious to us.

Tom Lopez, a Chumash man in his forties, says that the way he was treated varied. Talking about his white friends, which included local Irish and Danish individuals, he tells me that he didn't feel much social distance with them and that "growing up in the valley for us was fun; we were kids and had wide-open spaces back then." And yet, while he says, "We weren't really thinking racial prejudice very much," he also tells how some "aggies" and even teachers would joke about his heritage. "Most of them, when you told them you were native, they just kind of laughed. 'How can you be native with a Mexican surname or a Spanish surname?'"

Other Chumash and Latinos in their thirties remember outright racism in the classroom and the sports field, as well as the occasional fistfight between students. Sometimes Chumash and Latinos would have to watch each other's backs, forming strong friendships in the process. As Tom says, "Some of the teachers were racist. I ran into it in Little League baseball. There was good and bad. You'd get a bad coach and then there were other coaches who were good."

Social Exclusion and the Curriculum

Exclusion and discrimination was tied to an absence of Chumash history in the curriculum of the Santa Ynez Valley Union High School. The only public high school in the valley, it has long been an important site of cultural reproduction for local culture and class relations in the area. Chumash and Latino kids mix with white ranch kids, and this is where the history of the valley is taught and the inclusion or exclusion of different ethnic groups really matters.

As Adelina relates, "There was a bias against the reservation. And there is still a big bias. If you go to school they won't teach this culture—their own backyard—they won't teach the culture here. They'll teach the Navajo culture and all those other cultures that are in the east, and we're not in the east. Here you got the Yokuts, Chumash, all kinds of Indian people." When local history does get taught, it is about the Spaniards and the Gold Rush, and the Indians are mentioned only in the context of the missions. Language apprentice Tom Lopez puts it bluntly, telling me, "Chumash kids are treated different. They're still prejudiced towards the Indian kids. And they need to teach valley kids where the Chumash are coming from." When I ask Niki Sandoval if she ever saw herself or her people in the curriculum of the high school and grade schools in the valley, she responds emphatically, "No, absolutely not. Never."

Leslie Koda, former director of the American Indian Scholars Program at UCSB, attributes this absence of Chumash history to a general ignorance of teachers and administrators at the high school and throughout the public education system.

They just don't understand native people; it's not in the curriculum. The Indian kids themselves don't see themselves in the curriculum, and so they are not interested. "Where am I and where are my people?" And the general population in the school doesn't see that either, so there's no way for them to know and educate themselves and be supportive. And the only thing they hear is from their parents, which is, you know, the Indians and the casino, and they hear that at home and they regurgitate at school and then they pick on the Indian kids.

Many others, including Freddy Romero, share this view. He says that his daughter, while having some friends, often felt ostracized because of her Chumash background and being associated with the reservation. Freddy takes the teaching of history in the valley and throughout California to task. He finds the way in which most students in California learn about the missions and build mission dioramas in the fourth grade to be traumatic for native students.

Having all the kids build missions, that's like asking Jewish kids to build a replica of Auschwitz or the furnaces that they used to burn their people in. Did they do that at the mission? No, but it was almost as bad—they killed the culture. We didn't want to build missions; we were enslaved to build the missions. We were forced to do that or if not, we died. Others chose to run away from that and hide. Those that fled left their families and cultures, their relations behind. Most Indians lived near water sources, and most gold was found in creeks and rivers. "They're just damned Indians, savages, we'll just kill them." So we were always being displaced.

He and others feel that if this history were taught in the high school and if teachers were sensitive to the native perspective, the Chumash and other native students would embrace school and there would be less tension and more understanding among different ethnic groups.

Social Exclusion and "Tracking" Students
Another important consideration is the way Chumash students were tracked through school by teachers and administrators and the low

educational expectations held by teachers and parents. "Tracking" refers to the expectations surrounding individual students and the ways that teachers and counselors do or do not direct students to college-prep classes and college counseling. My interviews reveal a longstanding pattern that has consistently worked against the Chumash going on to college. Dominica Valencia, in her fifties and a long-time member of the Education Committee, speaks for several generations of Chumash when she tells me, "When we went to high school, the counselor would advise us to do labor work, house cleaning, and they didn't see any potential in us going to college, so they didn't spend much time advising us, how to get to college, even to junior college."

Niki Sandoval, who has both personal experience and a professional interest in the topic of tracking, went to college and eventually received her doctorate in spite of her experience at Santa Ynez Valley Union High School. She says, "I was never put on a college preparatory track, so college was something I had to investigate and pursue on my own, learn things the hard way, make mistakes. I didn't have the academic preparation to put me on a higher education path." Niki confirmed that there were low expectations for Chumash kids.

> The things you read in textbooks about educational inequities for low-income students and students of color not being considered for a higher academic track are true. Gifted and talented programs were something I knew nothing about. I saw a disproportionate number native students in our community placed in special education for no reason that I could see. Special ed was segregated in these little trailers kind of off in the perimeter of the campus in the elementary schools. So you're talking about educational segregation happening in the late seventies, early eighties, and you can even argue into the late eighties, when I was a high school student.

How did labeling occur? Niki says,

> Speaking from my own observations, there was this assumption—and this is something that is corroborated by people I have interviewed in different generations in our community—that

the Indian kids were not into school, were not viewed as being capable of going into the higher academic track (and of course there was the occasional exception to that rule), but they were not really viewed as college material. And I know that because I never had a college counselor or teacher in my high school ever say the word 'college' or 'university' to me—ever!

Her sister Carmen, now one of the Chumash language apprentices, fared even worse. "From personal experience, it was difficult to live in the valley as a native child; I remember being labeled and put in special education classes just because I was native." She says that in the third grade, only reservation kids and mentally challenged kids were in special ed. At one point, she questioned one of the special education teachers.

"Why am I here?" "Well, your teacher recommends that you need to follow up with your reading skills and English skills because you are falling behind." I told her, "I am falling behind because I'm not in class; I'm in this class." So they would pull me out of class to go to special ed class, and then I'd do the work and then just sit there and wait. "What am I supposed to do? I've done the work!" And one time I took a test and I asked her if she could grade it. And she graded it and I got an A on it, and again I asked her, "Why am I being put here? I finished under time and my grade seems to be good." And she said, "Honestly, Carmen, I don't know why you are here." It lowered my self-esteem. "Well, okay, they're only going to expect this out of me, so why should I go? If this is how they see me, so why try? I don't have to." So from then on school was not my priority. My priority was working and earning money. And putting money towards the house—my mother was a single mom raising four girls. I worked full-time throughout my high school years. I had more work hours than school hours.

Carmen's experience in elementary school was shared by other Chumash youth in the 1980s, as a disproportionate number of native students were placed in special education. In sum, educational forces in these years worked against many Chumash students from pursuing education past the high school level.

This pattern was experienced by Chumash at other schools in the larger Central Coast region. For example, Frances Snyder, one of the few other Chumash to have gotten a postgraduate degree until recently, states how hard it was to overcome the odds, both at school and in her family. Frances, part of an "Indopino" family—that is, part Indian (in this case Chumash) and part Filipino—grew up off-reservation in Arroyo Grande, forty-five minutes north of the valley.

> When I was a teenager, my parents expressed surprise that I was interested in college. Their goal for me was to finish high school, get a job as a secretary, and marry young. They didn't know that college was a possibility. In fact, my father told me that college was for rich white boys—not for the economically disadvantaged, not for people of color, not for girls. He wasn't trying to be discouraging. That's simply the way things were back in those days. When I did it, my parents were extremely proud and very supportive—but it was a struggle for me, financially, culturally, and emotionally.

Frances was driven to go to college and succeed, she tells me, because she realized what an exception to the rule she was in her community. But her drive also came from the way she was slighted by a teacher in sixth grade. "Throughout grammar school and high school, I always felt as if I had to prove myself to my teachers. In sixth grade, I overheard one teacher talking to another teacher about me. 'Oh, her? She's just a Filipino pea picker's daughter. She'll be quitting school by the time she's thirteen and working out in the field.' It was shocking and hurtful, and I remember feeling as if I always had to prove these teachers wrong."

Education and Exclusion in the Valley Today

Tonie Flores contrasts her own experience in the high school back in the early '60s with changes in the school since then and with her grandchildren today. She does not remember Santa Ynez Valley Union High School fondly, and to this day she will not go back. Her dyslexia was not understood by the teachers, and she was put in a group with kids who could not read at all. She's surprised she graduated with her reading ability; many of the other

Chumash kids did not. She says that that the situation was different for her kids, now in their thirties, at the high school. Although they did face some antagonism and still felt class differences, they were popular in school and had many white and Latino friends, good social skills, and generally fit in. Part of this change she attributes to the changing ethnic composition of the valley, affected especially by the influx of Mexican immigrants.

Others have a different take on how the high school experience has changed over the last decades for the Chumash. When a housing boom began in the late '70s, things began to change socially in the valley, and that was reflected in the high school. Today it is different, according to Dominica Valencia, "because of the wineries, the people that have come in, outsiders. You know, when you have a farm worker working for a ranch, let's say, the kids back then got along; they didn't degrade each other. Now they go to school and say, 'Ha! You're wearing my hand-me-downs, your dad works for my dad.' And when you're in school, that really affects children because they don't realize that there's such a thing as social class."

Willie Wyatt agrees that there is still separation. "In some respects it's tougher now. Now we have this conflict in the Santa Ynez Valley over gaming, and the kids are having to deal with that now. It's separating the Native Americans and non-Indians on this issue. They hear things from their parents and they take those same attitudes to school." In short, social separation spills over into the classroom.

While Chumash educational initiatives and the newfound economic and political power of the tribe are altering the education of their youth, many students still have a bad experience that discourages them from pursuing higher education. Leslie Koda, who ran a mentorship program out of UC Santa Barbara for Chumash students at the high school, says that "there is tension, major tension there" among kids and in the general campus climate. "We asked one of the high school students we are mentoring what her interests are at the school, and she said, 'I just want to get the hell out of here.' How do you work with and change a student like that so they want to go on in school?" Negative experiences such as this even exist in elementary school.

So, although the new revenues and the educational programs are making college part of the conversation for Chumash kids, social separation continues today. Niki Sandoval tells me,

With this new infusion of the gaming revenue, I actually think in some respects it's harder socially for native students in our community because they have to contend with the social misconceptions that exist about the revenue. People might assume that they're wealthy, which isn't always the case. They assume that they have it easy or even that they get a free ride for college. So there's a lot of misinformation out there and that's why education is so important. That's why having some kind of indigenous education with the local school curriculum is so important, because people don't know our native past. They certainly don't understand our native present, and they have a lot of confusion and fear about the future.

Language apprentice Carmen Sandoval also talks about the ambivalent relationship that the larger community has with the tribe now that there is the casino wealth. She says that, before,

we got more grief from the teachers than from the students, and it was like, "Oh, you're from the reservation," like it was a bad thing. Now it's, "Oh, you're from the Rez?! How much money do you get? I've got a softball team—do you want to sponsor them? You're from the Rez?! Why do you drive that dirty old car? Why not a Mercedes Benz?" So that's what we get now. In pre-casino times, it would be, "You're from the reservation?" and you'd be cast aside. They'd instantly label us.

Niki agrees, saying,

There needs to be improved interpersonal relationships. I think that the power of friendship, fellowship, actual genuine connection between people without any other interests than making sure students have access to opportunities and can be successful are important. I'd like the focus to be on the students and our society and making things better for all people. But I think a lot of times, because of this infusion of gaming revenue, people see the dollar signs so there's a lot of mistrust on the part of native people because they're not sure if administrators or people on the PTA or teachers are all of a sudden interested in their kids just because they want the grant money, a new athletic program, they want this and that. So there's a lot of fear and mistrust on both sides.

In sum, little has changed in the curriculum or in the validation of American-Indian identity. But change is afoot. Niki and others are working to create not just better mentoring and tutoring but a more positive cultural climate in general for Chumash kids. They see a clear need to build relationships among school officials, parents, and the larger community, and the need to tell the Chumash story. In that sense, Chumash parents, grandparents, and families should be seen as cultural resources, Niki says. "Taking advantage of the human resources in our community, both on and off the reservation, is the key. Another is just acknowledging that there was a presence here with a great time depth which deserves some kind of acknowledgement in the things we do."

Fortunately, many Chumash educational programs are building relationships, many teachers and principals are increasingly receptive to these programs, and these changes are benefitting both Chumash and non-Chumash students, as we will see in the next chapter.

Five

Knowledge Is Power:
New Educational Opportunities

"We're also teaching them about feathers. They were given a red-tail-hawk feather and they were given it the right way. It wasn't, 'Hey, here's a feather.' It was prayed over. We talked about the bird, what parts of the bird our people used, what it means to us. And after we talked about its meaning, and after the meeting, a lot of the kids were pulling the feather out and just staring at it, looking at it. Because it meant more than just being a feather."

Nakia Zavalla, cultural programs director

It would be hard to overstate how much the casino revenues have benefited Chumash education and culture. A little-known fact in the wider Santa Ynez community is that the programs of the Chumash Education Fund are open not just to the one hundred and fifty or so members of the tribe, *but to descendants as well.* This is a huge benefit for the tribe, as the potential beneficiaries run through several generations and number upward of twelve hundred people—and growing. To date, several hundred people have taken advantage of the programs. Today, many more Chumash students are completing high school; many who had dropped out years ago are now getting their GEDs; grade and high school students have the benefit of strong tutoring and mentoring programs; the tribe has its own culturally appropriate youth summer program; Chumash youth and adults are getting computer classes and vocational school training; and through the Chumash Education Fund, many are now breaking through long-standing social barriers to get college degrees and beyond.

Moreover, in educating themselves, the Chumash are increasingly learning about their own history and culture, and they are also now teaching this to the larger community. They do this not only by challenging the curricula and faculty of local schools to teach their history, but by school visits, educational videos, and, in one case, the establishment of a personal museum.

The Chumash Education Department

The Education Department, housed in one of the wings of the large Tribal Hall, consists physically of a medium-sized room with a bank of computers by the office of the education programs director, a small tutoring room, a bathroom, and a teachers' lounge. Oftentimes a beehive of activity as students, tutors, and others come and go, it is one indication of how far the Chumash have come. Before the mid-1990s, there had been education programs, but they were modest in scope, often underfunded and short-lived. In 1994, when scholarships became available to all Chumash descendants—the number of which is growing with each new generation—a great many new educational opportunities opened up. In the late 1990s, the General Council—made up of all tribal members—voted overwhelmingly in favor of even more far-reaching education programs. Many Chumash today express pride that the tribe was so united on this important issue. In 2003, when the tribe hired an education programs director, a flurry of educational initiatives was enacted, and the careful nurturing of these diverse programs is now bearing significant fruit.

The Chumash Education Department is made up of the education programs director and the Education Committee, and it has a mailing list of several hundred Chumash individuals. When the late Fred Loveys was hired by the tribe in 2003 as the first education programs director, he and the committee put together a number of educational, recreational, and cultural programs, including a six-week summer program, an after-school tutoring and mentoring program, and many other activities that have engaged Chumash youth and adults alike. They also created effective educational partnerships with local K-12 schools, UC Santa Barbara, the Sedgwick Reserve, and the local YMCA. They have mentored students and conducted academic counseling for high school students, including youth at risk of leaving school. The Education Department also coordinates with the cultural programs director, the language apprentices, and other tribal committees. The Department interfaces with other American-Indian education programs, offers student advocacy and leadership development, parent education opportunities, family forums, academic skill workshops, and presents an annual graduation celebration. When Dr. Loveys died in 2009, the tribe hired Niki Sandoval as director, and her considerable expertise in tribal education has helped to further these programs as well as create new ones.

Today, education works for and not against culture. The tribe knows that improving education must be linked to strengthening Chumash identity, revitalizing the culture, and instilling cultural pride in its young people, and it has made a concerted effort to educate its youth about their history and culture. This expanded education program has created a spillover effect, and the Chumash are today educating not only themselves but also the rest of the valley about their culture and history.

Chumash Educational Programs

A percentage of the casino revenues are allotted to education programs, and a number of different programs as well as different funds are available to support all levels of education for all descendants of the tribal members. These recipients do not have to live on the reservation or in the area, although most do; some even live in other states. Those who live outside the area, however, do not benefit from the various support systems and programs sponsored locally, of which there are many.

One of the most successful has been the mentoring and tutoring program. Each student has access to tutorial services at the Tribal Hall, in their homes, or at the local library. Approximately thirty tutors offer individualized support in a wide range of academic subjects, from math, reading, and science, to English, social studies, and Spanish. The tutors are usually credentialed teachers from the local community.

Besides the tutoring funds and resources, the tribe provides significant funding for descendants' expenses for preschool, after-school care, and even private school. Given the ways many local schools have failed the Chumash in the past, some tribal members are opting for this alternative. Kathy Marshall says,

> These public schools are great compared to the ones in big cities. But for me going through what I went through, I know that even today it is so easy for kids to slip through the cracks. And I feel very comfortable sending my kids to private school because I feel that it doesn't happen there. You have small classes. You meet with the teacher more than once a year. They're always contacting you. My children are getting the education they deserve.

The general support that the kids get from the tribe is inspiring. Besides the annual back-to-school event in which the education department gives away backpacks and counsels students, there are also funds available to descendants for after-school activities such as ballet, singing, painting, piano, summer camps, and sports. Adult education—a separate funding category from college—is also supported by the tribe, and it takes many forms, including support for professional development, continuing education, seminars, workshops, and conferences. One descendant told me about his own continuing education before telling me about how excited his daughter was to be leaving soon for a college semester abroad in London. These kinds of educational opportunities, which are now flowing through several generations, were inconceivable even a short time ago.

College

Just as the tribe has provided a strong and well-funded support system for its youth in pre-school, grade school, and high school, so, too, is it readily supporting higher education for its young adults and adults. As we saw in the last chapter, in the past, those Chumash who did graduate from high school were not tracked for college, and few attended. This is consistent with Native Americans in general, who "have more difficulty attending college than most and for reasons that have nothing to do with the quality or capacity of individuals."

With increased support systems and funding, however, the number of college-educated Chumash has increased greatly. In 2005, the *Los Angeles Times* reported that "tribal subsidies have helped nearly 100 Chumash attend a university, community college, or trade school" (*LAT* 12/03/05). The number has risen greatly since then.

Through its generous and closely monitored funding program, the tribe provides support for college expenses such as tuition, books, registration, health insurance, and room and board. This is a tremendous potential benefit for the more than twelve hundred Chumash descendants and an important incentive that has motivated many Chumash youth to go on to college and adults to return to school. Chumash are being educated in many disciplines and a few are even gaining advanced degrees in prestigious fields of study, including law and medicine.

Another plus to the higher education program, according to Education Committee member Dominica Valencia, is that if recipients receive outside assistance, the tribe supplements the remaining balance. "To me and the committee, that's a plus because they're out getting scholarships, doing this and doing that for their benefit, to go to school." She goes on to tell me that when kids in college are struggling in a particular class, the Education Committee and education programs director monitor the situation, suggesting tutoring and other alternatives. The growing number of college graduates is a point of pride for the tribe.

A number of Chumash descendants have now pursued their studies past a bachelor's degree. Walter Viar, a descendant in his early thirties, received a BA from San Diego State University before taking a law degree from the University of San Diego. He says that the tribe's financial support made this possible. "When I first started college there weren't any scholarships available through the tribe, so I got five hundred dollars a semester for college my first year or maybe two years, and that wasn't so good," he tells me. He then goes on to describe how the tribe increased its funding for his college, covering a good part of his room and board, books, tuition, and travel expenses. "Without that funding, I probably wouldn't have been able to go to either school, or it would have been much more difficult. A lot of my friends graduated with tons of student loans; I came out without owing anything, which was so fortunate, especially considering the cost of law school." He went to work for a law firm specializing in American Indian law. And after taking culinary and language classes in Italy, using the adult education funds, he is increasingly interested in living abroad in Italy. But he may also come back and serve the tribe. He has a lot of dreams and a lot of alternatives. "As far as I'm concerned, education is one of the most important things. It's a springboard for everything."

Dolores Cross, Walter's aunt, makes it clear that the funds for higher education have benefited her entire family.

> Well, my niece has a children's shop, my nephew has his own business; my brother is a chef and has a café; my sister has a spa; my daughter has a business management degree. And my nephew is now working for Sony; he has two degrees. I don't think these kinds of opportunities would ever have happened. I don't know where we'd be; it was a struggle, my husband and I working full-time. Funding for college was very difficult back then, and my daughter took out a lot of loans. Now she can carry on in school if she wants.

Carmen Sandoval says that after working in the food and beverage industry, she decided to return to school with the help of higher education funds from the tribe and other grants. She got into the medical field, first obtaining a certification for ultrasound at a private college and then her AA from Santa Barbara City College in the radiologic technology program. "I was never really big on school, but now I'm very focused—I was honored with outstanding student for my graduating class at City College!" Today, Carmen is doing contract work up and down the coast for different imaging centers. But she is also involved with the tribe, as a language apprentice and as a native monitor. She is planning to return to school to pursue a degree in anthropology in order to communicate with archeologists and be more effective at site preservation and as a liaison between the tribe and the larger community.

For Niki Sandoval, the funds were not available for her BA or most of her MA degree. Before returning to California to pursue her PhD, she worked at the Smithsonian Museum for a decade. For her PhD, the education funds were decisive. "When I was figuring out if I wanted to do my PhD, that was one of the factors that helped stimulate me to go, because if there was not that support there's no way I would have given up a lucrative career to focus on school. But still I am probably going to be paying back the student loans from my bachelors and masters until I'm sixty!"

College was not part of the picture for Willie Wyatt initially. When he was growing up, his father worked as a ranch hand and his mother held down various jobs to support the family. But after doing several menial jobs, Willie decided to go to college. He first went to DQ University (Deganawidah-Quetzalcoatl University), a Native American junior college in northern California, before getting his BS from UC Davis. About that time, the tribe had scholarships that paid the better part of tuition and living expenses and that eased the burden. Together with student loans, he was able to complete his degree. "If I had not received the scholarships, I would have a lot more student loan debt." He finished in 1997 and came back because he wanted to apply what he had learned in his own community. The Environmental Protection Agency was offering grant funds to tribes to develop environmental programs, and Willie became the first tribal environmental manager for the Chumash. He is now the tribal administrator.

One of the most eloquent testimonies of what the casino revenues have meant in a person's life comes from Gwendolyn Kilfoyle, a Chumash descendant in her mid-twenties, who spoke at the annual Chumash Graduation Awards Ceremony in 2005. First taking her AA degree from Santa Barbara City College, she had just completed her BA in psychology at Sonoma State University. She was planning to attend a graduate program in counseling to become a licensed family and marriage therapist.

> An education at a liberal arts college has also given me confidence in my ability to form ideas, concerns, and beliefs using critical thinking. In giving the gift of a quality education, the tribe as represented by the Education Committee and Education Department serves its individual members, the integrity of the tribe as a whole, and our local communities, which benefit from having educated and skilled professionals. Speaking on behalf of myself and my generation and the generations to come, I thank you for making this a priority in your budget and your work. I look forward to repaying you through the contributions I make, leading to a healthier, saner, and more peaceful world.

Parents and Schools as Support Systems

Money provided for higher education is of no help to the tribal children unless there are support systems in place, both at home and at school. Much educational research, including that of Chumash scholar Niki Sandoval on the reservation, shows that family involvement is crucial to positive educational opportunities and outcomes. Parents and the extended family have to be involved in teaching and learning not only to encourage school-based education but to share their own knowledge about Chumash history and culture. Just as important is support and direction in the local schools. Although the tutoring and other education programs help Chumash students, there are still enough antagonistic forces at home and at school to turn many Chumash youth away from pursuing higher education and sometimes even from graduating from high school.

To reach the goal of increased parental and school support, the American Indian Scholars Program was established at UC Santa Barbara in 2006. Leslie Koda, former director of the program, says that the goal is to give students as many options as possible and to keep them in school and in higher education. "We want to connect with the kids and get Chumash kids going to college, furthering their education, be it vocational school, community college, or CSU or UC." To this end, although Leslie works at all levels, the program has put most of its energy into the high school. The program funds a number of mentors, who are UC Santa Barbara undergraduates, for Chumash and other American-Indian youth at the high school. Each student is assigned a mentor and is assisted in planning academic preparation, raising grades and tests scores, and selecting classes. The mentors guide students toward and through classes needed for UC eligibility, help them find out what financial assistance is available, and make sure they also work with their counselors at the school.

The idea is to build a cohort of mutually supportive students, to improve relations between students and their teachers and counselors, and to demystify the academic process, including how to get into college. All these activities are connected to the home. The program engages parents and the extended family of individual students, implementing "an academic language within the home." Leslie states that the goal is to empower the parent. "Maybe the parents have not finished even fifth grade. Do they feel like they can talk to their son or daughter that's in high school, such as asking them, 'Hey, what are you studying in math?' Or 'What is that reading for?' You know, there are some parents that don't even feel like they're able to ask those questions. But because they are parents they are role models and can be mentors, and they need to know they can step into those positions." Parents, she tells me, need to take an active interest and participate in back-to-school night and teacher/parent conferences, as well as feel comfortable expressing concerns.

Another key goal is to promote dialogue between students and elders through a multigenerational learning program. Elders are invited to talk to students about Chumash culture, their relationship with the earth and with sacred sites, and indigenous contributions to science and other areas of knowledge. "In essence we bring culture into the classroom. If we can't reform the curriculum in the schools, we have to feed it to the students in other ways."

Chumash Education Director Niki Sandoval also stresses the importance of viewing parents, grandparents, siblings, and the extended family as cultural resources.

> There are the language apprentices, people who know about music, survival skills, traditional instruments, baskets, cultural traditions. With baskets they can teach not only environment history and culture, but math, and it cuts across disciplines. To see the opportunities for learning, and recognize that people still possess that knowledge. You might not see it on the surface—the person might be wearing their button-down shirt, tie, and slacks because they have an office job during the day. They might have knowledge that you are not aware of until you connect with them. Taking advantage of the human resources in our community, both on and off the reservation, is the key. Another is just acknowledging that there was a presence here with a great time depth which deserves acknowledgement in the things we do.

There are efforts to do just that, whether it's pressuring Sacramento to change the curriculum, improving support systems for kids, or trying to provide a positive cultural climate within the schools themselves. Sometimes native faculty from UC Santa Barbara is brought in to present lectures. "Now you're getting high school students saying, 'You learned that at college? Well, I want to learn it here!' And then we approach the superintendent or principal and say, 'Hey, what can we work out here to help these students learn?'"

Leslie says that the principals at all of the schools have been uniformly receptive to the American Indian Scholars Program, and increasing numbers of teachers are cooperating. For those teachers who resist the program, Leslie believes that "they will feel relief when Native American kids are doing better in their classes, and when conflict and tension between Chumash and non-native kids gets defused. They, too, will come around."

Education and Identity

Until recently, the educational system worked against Chumash identity. Not only did it not teach or valorize Chumash culture, but school-based education perpetuated the erasure of Chumash history and culture. And, socially, at school, the Chumash kids were often made to feel ashamed of being from the reservation. Since the 1990s, something of a turnaround has been spearheaded by the Chumash themselves. Today, education and cultural identity are coming together in dynamic ways.

As we saw in the last section, Chumash educational initiatives presently are often linked to the valuing of Chumash and American-Indian identities, whether it is visiting authors, elders sharing stories with youth, or attempts to alter the curriculum at the state and local levels. Many of these initiatives overlap with the cultural programs, such as the Samala Language Apprentice Program, the Chumash Dictionary Project, and Camp Kalawashaq, detailed in the next chapter.

Cultural education, whether supported by tribal or state funding on the reservation or in local schools, used to be very limited. Funds were minimal, especially compared with the money that today is being poured into cultural education by the tribe and individual families. Kathy Marshall, speaking about the programs run by the cultural revitalists in the 1970s and '80s, says, "I have spoken to people who helped our elders receive grants, and from what I understand they were in amounts of three hundred dollars or less, not large at all. So it's amazing to me how things have evolved because three hundred dollars nowadays wouldn't get you your beverages," she tells me, laughing. "So the casino revenues opened up so many doors for us. You hate to mix culture with money, but you can't avoid it because you have to feed the people, you have to have a place to have the people, have your ceremonies. It has definitely changed it. We are going strong, and it's awesome."

On the reservation, cultural education includes regalia-making, basket-weaving, culture nights, "culture as prevention," and language classes in the Samala language. The Tribal Hall is the setting for many of these programs. For example, on the Monday night "Culture Night," a cultural presenter teaches a new skill, such as basket-making, beading, rock art, regalia-making, and storytelling. These culture nights as well as other cultural workshops given in the hall are generally well attended, with twenty or more individuals, often parents with their children, showing up on any given night. Besides the teaching of culture, Nakia Zavalla says that it also "gives a sense of community." All cultural events such as this begin with a prayer thanking the creator, and often traditionalist Adelina Alva-Padilla or another Chumash elder will be present to burn sage and "sage" the participants, by blessing them individually by bathing them with its smoke.

Many of the Chumash involved with education tell me that "culture is prevention" in the sense that an absence of cultural knowledge and pride is often linked to alcoholism and drug abuse. Cultural and historical knowledge increases identity and self-esteem, which can work against self-abuse. The Daughters of Tradition and Sons of Tradition programs, which foster cultural pride and self-respect among native youth, are held at the reservation and in other youth forums, such as in Camp Kalawashaq. Meetings at the reservation are on Friday nights, because, as Nakia says, that's the night kids get into trouble. "So the community supports them in making healthy choices. It's all based off the creator, putting the creator first, having respect for yourself, your elders, your community. That's why we have it, to give thanks to the creator, to build character, to have that compassion for others."

Another way in which cultural programs are fostering cultural pride is through the Language Apprentice Program, in which five Chumash individuals are being trained in the language and are in turn bringing the language into diverse forums in the community. Established in 2007, the language apprentices have been teaching the Samala language in youth classes at the Tribal Hall. They are already having a profound effect. As apprentice Carmen Sandoval says,

I've had parents come up to me and go, "Wow, my kids are just singing and singing their little hearts out. What does that song mean?" These children are sparking that interest in their parents, to ask that question, so then that parent can get that information and go home and really understand it. Something triggers it in them; it can be just one song, one color they can identify with, and then they know what that color is in Samala. I play my tapes in my car and my son is there while I'm driving. He also goes to classes but we have incorporated it into our daily lives.

The language apprentices have also been making an impact in the class-rooms of local schools. Kathy Marshall says,

I think it adds a lot. We started doing presentations at schools. If there is a Chumash student in the group that we're teaching, their faces light up, like, "Yeah, that's me. That's where I belong; those are my people." And it happens at every school when there is a Chumash kid in the crowd, and it's just an awesome thing to see. We went to the first grade at Solvang School and two Chumash kids were in the group. When we started singing, their faces looked so proud. A lot of the other students think that we still live in Tule huts or teepees. They have a lot of questions; they want to know.

In addition to her duties as a language apprentice, Kathy has been work-ing hard at the state level on the American Indian Education Oversight Committee.

I've learned about the history and the opportunities that are out there for our tribe. I think we are pretty secluded in Santa Ynez because there's not a lot of tribes around us that are federally recognized and get the grants that all these tribes do. There's a lot of grants out there for us that we have not tapped into yet. Being on this committee has opened those doors for me. Not only that but I have made so many new contacts that have really helped with our tribe.

Participating in curriculum review at the state level is a new adventure for the Chumash. When I ask Kathy if this opportunity would have happened without the casino revenues, she replies with an ironic laugh, "No way. We wouldn't be where we are right now. I would not be on this committee, and Jack O'Connell [California state superintendent of public instruction] would not have phoned Chairman Armenta himself, saying, 'There needs to be representation in your area.' Without having the casino funding, this opportunity would not have arisen, and that's a fact."

The casino wealth and the education funds generated by it are helping to educate the Chumash about the larger issues facing American Indians as a whole. For example, many Chumash are raising their cultural and political awareness by using their adult education funds to go to conferences and workshops elsewhere in California and in other states, and by sharing experiences back home. These meetings provide knowledge about health issues, budgets, day care, and other programs in "Indian country." Dominica Valencia says that things are run differently in Indian country, that tribal peoples face particular problems, and that it really helps to network with different native nations. "I meet people from Alaska, Oregon, Washington, Oklahoma, Arizona, Utah. It's kind of neat to talk with them because we all kind of have the same problems. It's just on a different level—politics all the way from A to Z. Sometimes we find an answer to our problem."

Freddy Romero has been sent by the elders to become educated in historical preservation law, so that he is able to understand and speak to issues having to do with Chumash cultural patrimony. He has participated in the President's Advisory Council for Preservation, received NAGPRA (Native American Graves Protection and Repatriation Act) training from the National Park Service, and has traveled to Washington, DC, Arizona, and Washington State for conferences related to cultural preservation and development on Native American land.

The experiences of Kathy, Dominica, and Freddy are illustrative of how, at an institutional level, many Chumash individuals are expanding their knowledge to benefit the tribe. Also, because of their newfound wealth, many Chumash have the means and the time today to research and learn about their history and culture. Niki Sandoval tells me, that in the past, "historians and anthropologists would write things and never show them to the Chumash." Now the Chumash are able to hire anthropologists and linguists to bring back and monitor and control that cultural information.

"We have more urgency now and are not so hesitant to contact people who have done a lot of research. We are a very well documented people and the resources are out there, but now we are getting a better understanding as a people that we have ownership in that we now have the ability to change that record and make it right. And I hope that stimulates a new generation of scholars and doers and thinkers to start adding to the knowledge base. The more people learn, the more they want to be part of that record keeping."

Reggie Pagaling feels similarly. He says,

There are hundreds of books written by non-Indians, without our participation, that shape outsiders' views of us. It has always been from one perspective. And a lot of these books exist and are available in museums and libraries but are not part of the educational system; they have never lent themselves to helping this culture or helping Native Americans in particular understand what they've gone through. They've been used by outsiders completely. With our participation, that's changing. We're totally involved now.

It all comes back to self-esteem, cultural pride, and identity. Dominica Valencia states,

When my grandmother was a little girl, they told her not to speak Chumash. And so that's why the language was lost and the culture. And now the tribe has brought it back and felt it important that our youth understand our culture; that it's still here and it's still alive, because a lot of our youth are lost because they go off to other tribes and, "They still have this, they still have that, their dances," and when they come to us, what do we have? I always think the children were lost and they need something stable, some kind of security, to know who they are and where we come from. I think that's important for everybody, not just natives, everyone. We want to know who we are and where we come from. That's a way to give them confidence: "You know what? We are Chumash, and, yes, we do have a culture and, yes, we do have a language."

100

Niki Sandoval says,

> Cultural education opportunities, the summer enrichment
> programs, the social activities have created a more cohesive
> community. It's had rippling effects. It's not only helped
> continue cultural practices in our community, which is very
> important, but also serves as the glue which binds people
> together. It helps people form an identity that is positive and
> rich, and I know that it is made possible by funding. I could
> sit here and tell you, "No, no, no, we were always like that,"
> but when Mom and Dad are working two or three jobs, they
> don't have time to go to the Tribal Hall on a Thursday night
> and show someone how to make regalia or lead a song for a
> ceremonial occasion. So it would dishonest to say the revenues
> didn't have any kind of impact.

The Future

The many educational opportunities that have opened up for the
Chumash in both mainstream education and Chumash cultural programs
have changed educational opportunities dramatically. These extend
beyond the tribe to the local community and beyond. From the Chumash-
sponsored tutors at the high school and the work of the language apprentices educating grade school students throughout the county, to Chumash
reviewing curricula at the state level and traveling between states to
attend workshops, it is clear that the casino revenues have changed the
education equation considerably. The attention that Chumash youth now
receive from universities, the state government, and other institutions
such as museums is an indication of their newfound political and economic clout.

But as one Chumash man puts it, it's not just a question of money, but
of heart.

> We're still fighting for who we are. We're fighting for who we
> are every day. We're a bigger adversary; we have money behind
> us. We can hire attorneys and work at that level now, but for
> us personally it still comes down to our passion, what's inside
> of us. Because it doesn't matter if you have the money—if you

don't have the heart or the passion, you're not going to get your message across.

This combination of heart and financial resources has allowed the Chumash to overcome a long history of educational marginalization, which at a personal level is related to self-esteem and life possibilities. When I ask Tonie Flores to compare the educational opportunities available to her children and grandchildren today with those of the old days, she sighs and the tears well up. She takes off her glasses to wipe her eyes. "There's a future now, a future for them. They will not struggle like we did. The way I thought about myself in the sixties, I didn't feel good about myself, and it just really cut down my self-esteem. So the reason I cry is because now these kids can feel good about themselves, get educated, and be smart and a part of the world."

Joe Talaugon, another elder, voices similar sentiments when I ask him what Chumash education will look like twenty years from now. "I think it is going to be fantastic. Everything is leaning towards learning, learning, learning." He tells me that there will always be interference, with some people doing drugs and messing around.

> But the ones that stick with it and learn culture are the ones that are going to carry it on. In twenty years you're going to see a whole new Chumash community, with more culture involved. People are going to be more aware of who they are. If you are ashamed of being an Indian or you're ashamed of some of the things that happened to your parents or what have you, it's not good because you're not living a full life. Once I became aware of who I am and where I came from, who my ancestors were, I can walk into any room and speak to any group without any feeling of insecurity. It gives you a sense of pride, of strength. That's the most important thing.

Let's let Niki Sandoval—who has closely studied education on the reservation—have the last word.

> We're a native people and there is a rich and beautiful history we are part of. It is something special to be celebrated and not swept under the rug. Assimilation isn't necessarily the best goal you can have. You can be native and you can be successful in the

outside world. You can choose not to stay in the community. You can choose not to work for a tribal enterprise. You can pick another profession off the reservation and still be who you are, still make your family and community proud of you and make a contribution to society. You can be all of those things. You can walk simultaneously in more than one world. That is why it's so important to invest in culture and education.

Six

Cultural and Linguistic Revitalization

"There was a moment when they were doing their regalia and Carmen took the other kids aside who weren't working on the regalia and she was telling them stories, the story of the forgotten woman of the island. And she was singing the song. She asked, 'Does anyone know the song?' And one little girl raised her hand, a little six year old, and she started it with a rattle and she started shaking it. And this little tiny boy started singing the song. It still brings tears to me right now. And I thought to myself, 'Look at that. Maybe someday she is going to be carrying on with it'."

Virginia Garcia, adult mentor, Camp Kalawashaq

The previous chapter showed that education has been transformed by the casino revenues. Educational initiatives are increasingly tied to culture and identity while at the same time providing opportunities for success in mainstream society. Indigenous identity and education are no longer opposed and mutually exclusive.

But what effects have the casino revenues had on indigenous cultural identity? Critics of the tribe often bemoan the great cultural loss that the casino has supposedly brought about. But Chumash culture had already been ravaged and suppressed for two centuries before the casino was built. In fact, its newfound political and economic power has allowed the tribal government itself—rather than particular families—to sponsor cultural activities and promote Chumash heritage. This power reverberates through culture at many levels.

Besides the recovery and revitalization of Chumash history, language, culture, and heritage reviewed in this chapter, cultural power has also increased. As explored in the next chapter, this refers to the increased power that the Chumash have over their cultural patrimony, in their government-to-government negotiations over culture with various public agencies, and on the cultural politics of the valley.

Although I am most interested here in tribal government-sponsored cultural initiatives, we will also look at how many Chumash individuals now have the time and means to carry out ceremony and to explore their history and culture, and how this affects indigenous identity today.

Culture Loss and Recovery

As touched on repeatedly in this book, the Chumash experienced tremendous cultural and linguistic loss through three successive waves of colonization in the nineteenth century. The early and mid-twentieth century was not any better. And yet Chumash culture has always been there, diminished in size but not in heart. As Adelina, the spiritual leader of the tribe, says, her cultural practices and revitalization initiatives build on the work of those who came before her. Previous leaders of the tribe, both spiritual and secular, gave the tribe tremendous strength.

> If you got one person saying ceremony, that's going to be strong. Ceremony is that you're going to pray, and if you know in your heart 'this prayer means a lot,' that prayer is going to be answered. If they hadn't been strong, you and I wouldn't be here talking—and I believe that. If they hadn't been strong back in the fifties and sixties, we wouldn't have any of this, the casino, education, cultural programs. That's what carried it forward.

Yet, despite this strength and the fact that certain cultural practices remained in a few Chumash families during the twentieth century, most Chumash culture and language was suppressed and lost until the late 1960s.

If, then, you were to graph the course of Chumash culture and language from its origins—the horizontal axis being time, the vertical one being cultural strength—you would see a continuous line from thousands of years ago to about 1800. There you would note a sharp spike downward. First with the Spanish missions, and later with the Mexican and then the white settlers, the line would continue declining and then fragment into smaller lines, as individual families took over the responsibility of cultural reproduction from the tribe, a previously sovereign political entity supported by a strong ritual complex.

Yet there were increasingly strong political and cultural pressures for even those families to renounce or hide their Indian identity and to speak Spanish (and, later, English as well). Although some families hung on to some parts of the culture, many Chumash descendants in Santa Barbara County did not and were assimilated. The last fluent speaker of *any* Chumash language died in 1965, and the last fluent speaker of Samala many years before then.

But in the early 1970s through the early '90s your graph would show a radical change in direction, the arrow-tipped line veering up sharply from the mid-'90s on. During the late '60s and early '70s, as we have seen, a wave of Native American pride swept Indian country and did a great deal to revive the culture. The rising line on the graph representing culture during the 1990s and beyond is due to the casino revenues. These have given tribal members and their descendants increased time to pursue language and cultural projects, and have allowed the tribe to become a powerful sovereign political entity once again, one that, as a corporation—rather than solely through individual families—can formally produce and promote Chumash culture.

Today, the Elders Committee and the Cultural Programs Department (established in 2005) are charged with overseeing cultural projects, often in coordination with the Education Department. The Elders Committee is empowered by the tribe to safeguard Chumash cultural patrimony and promote the recovery and use of Chumash culture. Elected every two years and with a minimum age of fifty, the elders oversee cultural resources, reburials, and native site monitors. The elders are also involved in increasing the cultural sensitivity of staff from the Park Service and other government agencies. They often film and document these initiatives. They also work with the summer program and with the language program. As one of the elders, Dolores Cross, puts it, "One of the responsibilities of the elders is to bring culture and traditions back to the tribe and remind them how important these are. Elders are focused on the culture, on keeping respect, and teaching the kids to be respectful." Both the Elders Committee and the Cultural Programs Department have budgets that have allowed a florescence of cultural projects that support language, ritual, and pan-Chumash revitalization.

Language Revitalization

One of the most obvious and important cultural impacts of the casino revenues has been on Samala, the Chumash language spoken by the Ineseño Chumash. Today, the language is being revived. Fortunately for the tribe, an eccentric anthropologist, J. P. Harrington (1884–1961), worked with an Ineseño Chumash woman, Maria Solares (1842–1923), in the early twentieth century and left thousands of pages of notes and transcriptions of the language, including songs, stories, and other cultural information. In the 1970s, Richard Applegate, who was a doctoral student in linguistics at UC Berkeley, came upon boxes of the original Harrington manuscript materials, which were written primarily in Samala with Spanish, as well as some English. He produced a grammar for his dissertation, compiled a dictionary, and wrote a number of scholarly articles about the language during the 1970s and '80s. In 2003, Applegate was hired by the tribe through its Education Committee to create a language program and revive the language. He was also commissioned by the Elders Committee to transcribe and translate thousands of pages in the Samala language that reveal a wealth of cultural information about the Chumash. He has also completed a beautiful Samala/English dictionary.

The revival of Samala is nothing less than remarkable. First, in spite of the pressures against her language and culture at the time, Maria Solares had been groomed as a culture-bearer by her great uncle, she was educated in the old Indian ways, and she spoke fluent Samala. She bridged two very distinct eras. Harrington's ex-wife, Carobeth Laird, tells us that Maria's grandmother "had been *esclava de la misión*. She had run away many, many times, and had been recaptured and whipped 'til her buttocks crawled with maggots. Yet she had survived to hand down her memories of the golden age before the white men came." Maria kept those memories alive and imparted them, as well as her own experience of the nineteenth century, to anthropologist Harrington in the 1910s. She spoke no English, according to Laird.

Second, it is amazing that it was the anthropologist Harrington who was able to find her in time. He was an inveterate researcher, and one of the most prolific gatherers of field data ever known. Both he and Laird were desperate to preserve what was left of native California. As Laird says, "The vessel of the old culture was broken and its precious contents were flowing away and evaporating before our very eyes. Harrington lapped like a man dying of thirst at every random trickle." His notes on the Chumash filled more than sixty boxes. Solares became one of Harrington's key informants, and they spent a lot of time together, she treating him "with the indulgence that one would accord a child or a harmless madman." Sharing her vast knowledge of the language and culture with him, they together produced thousands of pages of material about the language and culture. Harrington's transcription of her spoken Samala constitutes the first time Samala had been written down at any length.

Third, the fact that these materials, sequestered away for a half a century in a basement, were found by someone such as Applegate, and that forty years after that the tribe would have the financial wherewithal to hire Applegate and bring back the language, seems almost miraculous.

The language program established by Applegate and the tribe has been a success. Beginning with monthly classes offered to adults and youth, it soon took on a number of interrelated projects, including a Language Apprentice Program, the creation of a Samala/English dictionary, and the recovery of historical and cultural information.

Begun in 2003, the language program first involved teaching introductory classes, one for adults and one for children, in Samala. Sophisticated PowerPoint presentations by Applegate and a website have now benefited dozens and dozens of Chumash members and descendants who have taken Applegate's classes. For the last several years, he has been assisted by the Language Apprentice Program, which he initiated along with Nakia Zavalla in 2006. Nakia explains what motivated her: "Language is the key to unlock the door to all our cultural life and that's what we're finding out; without language it just doesn't work. Because we need the words for all these different things that we're using. And the children love it, they love the songs, and now they know what they are singing about."

The Language Apprentice Program

The apprentice program began with five of Applegate's most dedicated students: Nakia Zavalla, Carmen Sandoval, Kathy Marshall, Tom Lopez, and Frank Dominguez. In their thirties and forties, the language apprentices teach the language and Chumash culture to a larger group of students, both within the reservation and throughout the county.

Kathy Marshall, one of the apprentices, spoke to me about the program and what it means to the tribe.

> I thought, *It's just time.* I think that as far as language and culture we've kind of been a little stagnant for some years. You know, certain families kept their culture alive but just in their families. There weren't too many programs out there for our kids. Any tribe you go to and any native person you talk to, they tell you the language is the base. It is an awesome thing to see a Native American people speak their language. But it's been very difficult. It's a hard language to learn. Yet, above everything I am doing right now, that's where my heart is.

Carmen Sandoval, another one of the apprentices, says that the experience has been important for the tribe. "The language is within us, within our blood, our makeup as a person and a spirit, and it's just a matter of reigniting that. I personally try to work on it as much as possible because there's so many gifts in a language, not just to us personally but to us as a whole." She hopes that in the future people will be "taking the language into their everyday lives, using the language in their homes, in their prayer, in their songs. I see them conversing with one another, and a connection between the children and their grandparents. Some grandparents do remember the language, but it has been a long time since they heard it. So it's another wonderful and special connection between kids and grandparents."

The role of the elders in the apprentice program is extremely important. As Carmen puts it, "The elders are wonderful. They are so supportive and so genuine." Kathy adds that the language program has created a special bond among the apprentices themselves. "Now we have an elders board that is gathering all this and is willing to give it to the apprentices and so we're learning it and passing it on. They know we are doing it from our heart, this is who we are. And when we get together it's amazing because we know what we are doing."

Kathy continues,

> I think the gaming funds definitely have a lot to do with it because people before had to try and survive. Culture and language were not the priority. And no matter what you read, "You don't need money to have your culture"—in a way, that's true because it's in us—but on the other hand you do have to be able to hire your linguist. I think that Dr. Applegate in his heart would probably find some way to come out here on his own, but hiring people who have the knowledge which was taken from us is going to cost money.

Perhaps Nakia, the cofounder of the apprentice program, should have the last word.

> To me it's a dream come true. You hear other tribes talk their language and be fluent—for me as a young girl it was, "Gosh, I wish I knew how to speak my language," because my mom's generation was still coming out of the effects of the mission boarding school era. So now it's "Wow, we can actually say things, we can communicate with each other in full sentences." I didn't think it would happen in my lifetime. I'd say we're ahead of the game a little bit because the language was just about gone.

Samala Texts

In addition to providing information on vocabulary and grammatical structure, the texts that Harrington produced in collaboration with

Solares and others include "well over a hundred narratives in the Samala language. They range from tales of mythic times when the animals were still people to historical events such as the Mission Revolt of 1824 to descriptions of Chumash folkways such as childbirth practices." They describe medicinal formulas, cures, and daily activities such as fishing and gathering pine nuts. They contain historical accounts of life at the mission, personal experiences, and oral histories about various local figures, places, and events. These narratives also include greetings and conversations. They show various situations and personal interactions. They show people *using* the language in daily life. The narratives raise the language from being just a list of words and phrases; they bring it to life as a medium of communication.

The tribe commissioned Applegate to transcribe several hundred pages of unpublished texts from Harrington's research with Solares. This has yielded a tremendous amount of rich, new cultural information from the past. For the Chumash, most of whom are descended from Maria Solares, the narratives have special meaning. Kathy Marshall, the great-great-great-granddaughter of Maria Solares, tells me, "Ever since I got the narratives, I've just been gripped by them. I carry them in my car and read them any opportunity I have; I just want to know it all. So many stories about her grandfather and stories her grandmother told her, which date way back. It is just amazing—her experiences, her children, her life."

Carmen speaks of the value of the Harrington texts that are coming to light.

> Already we can understand certain customs. For many years there may be something in our daily life that we do, routinely, but you lose sight of the reason why you do it. What is wonderful now is that we know for a fact, wow, this is the reason. In general, we smudge [burning white sage and using the smoke for physical and spiritual cleansing] and there's many ceremonies and certain celebrations we do. But to have more information that could help support those even more is awesome. In general people categorize certain stories as 'lore,' but to our people these stories are real. Certain stories, like a creation story and why we have certain animals, why the woodpecker is the way it is, ocean life, from the whale to the

dolphin. These stories confirm why we honor certain animals, and also how our people saw them. So, you show respect for the hawk that's flying above, and we know that it is one of God's creatures. But did we really understand what it means to our people? So now we are able to read the stories, hear the stories, speak the stories in our language, to be able to educate our children and explain to their curious minds. Why does the crow sound like that? Why does the woodpecker store the acorns so high? Our children are inquisitive, so we are able to give them an explanation, a spiritual connection as well.

The Samala/English Dictionary and Language Recovery Today

A powerful new tool for the language program and for cultural revitalization in general is the *Samala/English Dictionary*, published by the tribe in 2007. This user-friendly dictionary, the culmination of Richard Applegate's work on the language, is not just a guide to the Samala language but a wonderful cultural resource that provides historical background, drawings, color photographs, and a great deal of linguistic and cultural information. Over six hundred pages in length, it is comprehensive, aesthetically pleasing, and a wonderful tool for language revitalization.

But this is not to say that the Chumash have recovered their language. Relatively few Chumash can say more than a few phrases, and they are still a long way from having a community where Samala is used in everyday speech. As Kathy Marshall says, in reference to the task of teaching Samala, "It's just a really hard thing to do. It's baby steps." She says that some people are intimidated by the different orthography and structure of the language, and teaching kids is a special challenge. "We try, first of all, songs. We have written songs, the kids have written songs, so that's a good way. I heard a woman from another tribe say, 'That's how we started, by just teaching them songs.' And then they go, 'Hey, I know that word.'"

Yet the use of Chumash has spilled over into many social venues. Today, Chumash words and phrases are used in prayer, song, to name children, and at graduation ceremonies and intertribal pow wows. The Chumash now know the names for their regalia, plants, animals, the meaning of place names, and much more.

As Applegate tells me,

> If I were of native blood it would be really important to me to
> know something of the language my ancestors spoke, even if I
> didn't speak it fluently. So that if I were out hiking and I saw
> a hawk, I'd know what my grandfather or great-grandfather
> might have called it. I think that for the tribe it is not so
> much an issue of reviving the language so that people will
> actually be fluent native speakers. But people can become
> proficient and even if they don't become proficient there is
> an incredible sense of identity that it helps to foster. The
> language apprentices told me that people are approaching
> them more often these days about creating songs or tying
> language in with other cultural projects, regalia, dances,
> rituals, and so on. Emotionally it is very powerful for them.
> I took a short text about woodpecker and the flood, and I
> recorded it at a sound studio. I played it at the first meeting
> of the students and one woman cried. She said it brought her
> to tears to hear it spoken again.

With the new dictionary, the language classes and apprentice program, and the transcription and translation of Harrington's Samala texts,
the Chumash have turned the tide against two hundred years of linguistic suppression. Applegate says that other Chumash groups, such as the
Barbareños and Ventureños, are also in the process of language recovery.
"But by far the Samala Chumash, the Santa Ynez Chumash, are doing more
with their language because they have the resources."

Ritual Revitalization and Cultural Heritage

Linguistic revitalization is one among several forces supporting cultural revitalization. The Chumash also now have access to the voluminous
historical and anthropological literature about them, and they are increasingly knowledgeable about their culture and history. With this knowledge,
many ritual practices, as well as dances, songs, stories, and plant knowledge, have been resuscitated or revitalized. Some ceremonies and cultural
activities are uniting the Santa Ynez Chumash with other Chumash groups

and even other Native American groups. Other ceremonies, such as that honoring Maria Solares, are altogether new.

Maria Solares

April 15, 2012, was a day for making history, with the premier of an original play produced by and about the Santa Ynez Chumash tribe. *Maria: An Original Play Honoring the Life of Maria Solares* illuminated a key figure in the tribe's history. Solares (1842–1923) was a beloved "grandmother" and learned culture-bearer, a venerable ancestor hero. This self-representation by and for the tribe represents an important and much larger shift in cultural awareness and power for the Chumash.

As we saw above, "most of what we know today about the Samala language and a great deal of what we know of the culture has been preserved because of Maria Solares's willingness to share her knowledge with Harrington." The head of a large family herself, compassionate and well-loved, she lived through a tumultuous time in Chumash history, dying at age eighty-one in 1923. Maria's father's parents came from Kalawashaq, the second-largest village in Ineseño territory. Born in 1842, Maria, as a child growing up in the valley, had the opportunity to know Chumash who were raised before the mission system. Her paternal grandfather was a religious leader who took part in the 1824 mission revolt. She married a man whose grandparents had come from the largest village in the valley, Soxtonokmu. Her father-in-law, Rafael Solares, was also a traditionalist and served as the chief of the Santa Ynez Chumash in the late 1800s. Her great-uncle would tell her stories about the Indian ways and she was groomed to be a culture-bearer.

Solares, then, is central to the tribe's history and heritage, and in 2007 the Chumash decided to honor her birthday with a large celebration. This was organized by the elders and by Cultural Programs Director Nakia Zavalla. The whole tribe was invited and the event was a success with over two hundred people packed into the Tribal Hall. More than one person has told me that it was the best-attended event there ever. With a large photo of Maria presiding over the gathering, the tribe had a big sit-down dinner, replete with storytellers, musicians, and dancers invited from other tribes, as well as prayers and songs, and Maria was thanked for her lasting legacy. Several of the elders with direct ties to Maria Solares were honored, and several of their older grandchildren went on stage and gave a brief history of Maria, while others recited stories that relate to her. Kathy Marshall says,

> We taught the kids some songs so they went up and sang them. And then Carmen and Nakia and I went up and we sang. It was actually the first time that we had gotten together to sing like that. The elders really pushed "Amazing Grace" in our language, and at first, I thought, Let's sing traditional songs. "Amazing Grace" is really not a part of us. But then Dr. Applegate translated it and we sat together with him and went through it to make sure it worked. After we sang it together for the first time, we were like, "Wow, that was pretty amazing!" It felt very powerful.

When I ask Tonie Flores about the Maria Solares celebration, she gets emotional:

> To honor her—there's no words. I honor her myself because she left a legacy. And if it was not for her we would have been lost, we would have lost this reservation in the long run, simply because we would not know who we are. Remember, we were told not to speak Chumash. We were told to become Catholics, to totally turn away from our beliefs, to speak Spanish. That's why we speak Spanish. And if it wasn't for her, we would have nothing.

The Ramada and Bear Ceremonies

Another instance of ritual renewal and ceremony dedicated to preserving tribal identity and cultural heritage is the Ramada Ceremony, which was brought back by the elders in 2003, after having died a couple of decades earlier. A *ramada*, a long, wooden structure covered with tree branches, is built in back of the Tribal Hall for this occasion. As Chumash elder Joe Talaugon tells me, it's about creating community. "Every year we bring the families together to exchange and meet each other, try to create some kind of family unit, because although everybody is related, they don't always know each other." Adelina, the spiritual leader of the tribe, opens with a prayer. Some wear regalia; there is a big potluck meal and singing.

Another ceremony that the Chumash do for themselves is the Bear Ceremony, which is held annually at the Tribal Hall or at other locations and can last several days. Joe explains to me that it is not really a Chumash ceremony and that it comes from the Yokut People. "Nevertheless, the Chumash and the Yokuts were very close and they exchanged a lot. The Bear Ceremony is a healing ceremony where the bears go to be a strong spirit; if people have problems, they're sick, have mental or alcohol problems, the bear ceremony helps you get cured and get through it. It's a healing process." The elders also sponsor a dinner for veterans every November, a Christmas celebration, and other events.

Pan-Chumash Revitalization and Beyond

There are currently revitalization movements in other Chumash groups that do not benefit from the casino revenues. This revitalization takes many forms, such as coastal Chumash reviving the *tomol* crossing, the recovery of language, and more people doing ceremony, basket-weaving, and other forms of material and nonmaterial culture. Have the casino revenues helped the Santa Ynez Chumash's relationship with these non-casino tribes and their cultural revitalization projects? In a word, yes. Although there has at times been tension among these different groups of Chumash, the Santa Ynez band's newfound economic power has allowed them to contribute to a wider pan-Chumash revitalization of culture and identity. Two clear examples are the solstice ceremony and the *tomol* crossing.

The Solstice Ceremony

The solstice ceremony was revived by different Chumash groups during the initial push for cultural revitalization back in the late 1960s and 1970s. In 2007, Pete Zavalla and Bobby Conno took several of the apprentices and elders to Sapac Si, a sacred mountain in the Sierras. They all camped in this remote area, aided by Pete Zavalla's knowledge of the area and work in the Forestry Department. There they did a summer solstice ceremony in a beautiful sacred area where there are rock and cave paintings, one of which has a painted sun on its ceiling, hence the name Sapac Si, "house of the sun." The ceremony, which was reserved for just a small group of people from the Santa Ynez Band, was a passing of the baton of sorts. Pete and Bobby had been doing the ceremony for a long time, as Kathy describes it. "They made sure we understood it's important to keep this tradition going. And in their own way they were saying, 'We're getting older and it's important that other people carry through,' and so I felt really honored."

The day after they returned from this ceremony, several of the language apprentices and elders, along with a number of Chumash youth, went to Mount Pinos for another solstice ceremony, one that is pan-Chumash, with individuals from other Chumash groups coming from as far away as Ventura and Bakersfield. Richard Applegate, who was also invited to this ceremony, says, "Mount Pinos was considered the sacred center of the Chumash cosmos and is the highest peak around. It's a way of bringing the entire nation back together. It's building community, and it's creating a richer sense of cultural identity."

Describing what it meant to gather pine nuts and do ceremony, Kathy says, "One of the stories Maria Solares tells is that they would go up to Mount Pinos and would do a celebration there for the summer. And part of what we learned from her stories is that you don't raise your voice, there's no ruckus, you're just really calm. It was just amazing, to know and feel what Maria Solares went through when she was there." Together they prayed and spoke of the importance of the place and ceremony to the Chumash. Many Chumash, dressed in their regalia, sang and danced, and there was a storyteller. Kathy says, "The evening was unforgettable and I will make sure that my children understand the importance of these places and these ceremonies."

The Tomol Crossing

Another important venue for intertribal solidarity and cultural revitalization is the *tomol* crossing, a Chumash activity that had not taken place for a century and a half until a group of coastal Chumash revived it in 2001. A rotating four-to-five-man crew paddles a traditional Chumash wood-plank canoe across the often treacherous twenty-one miles from the mainland at Oxnard to Santa Cruz Island. Two Santa Ynez Chumash are usually paddlers. Hundreds of supporters from coastal and valley Chumash, as well as others who come from as far away as the East Coast, camp on the island to receive the paddlers. Reggie Pagaling, a Chumash man who is in his mid-fifties, solidly built with graying ponytail and expressive face, tells me, "Paddling across gives a large community a base by which to rally. They stay on the island prior to our arrival there. They camp out days in advance—elders, children, young people, members of the community at large. It's been a way to unify, provide prayer and spiritual support for the group that is paddling across."

Reggie, who moved back to the valley in the late 1970s and who worked in education with the tribe in the '80s and '90s, says,

> It's a huge slice of me, of my mind, my body, my soul, from the concept of working with native peoples and actually building tomols. Working with those people building them, blessing them, paddling them, and reintroducing maritime skills by deed not by voice, which is totally different. You actually have that bond and understanding, the feeling of bringing something to life that was part of your ancestors. As you paddle, the experience over time puts you in a place where you feel each movement of the board, each pull of the paddle. And that's a point of unique spirituality because you can get so fatigued, you're tired, you hurt. Then you talk to the new paddlers, the ones that are learning about maritime skills and about our ancestors, and about saying, "Don't worry about the pain, that's long gone."

The trip itself is hazardous. The *tomol*, made, without nails, of redwood planks and stitched and glued with pine pitch and asphaltum, is thirty feet long, three feet wide, and two and a half feet deep, and weighs eighteen hundred pounds. With construction such as this, there are leaks, and the four-man crew is usually supplemented by a fifth, preferably small, person to bail water. They leave at four in the morning, and the crossing takes anywhere between nine and fourteen hours. Even with support boats and the switching out of paddlers every couple of hours, the journey is exhausting and hazardous. Battling strong currents, wind, waves, and large container ships, the *tomol* sits only a couple of feet above the water line. Reggie tells me that he calls the crossing a "promises trip." "I promise to be better to my kids, to my friends, to my wife. We make our promises because we realize that we are in a very dangerous situation; even the rescue crews have a difficult time assisting you if something goes wrong."

When I ask Reggie about the historical and cultural significance of the crossing, he stresses that it is about family and about culture:

> Heart and soul and community. Not all tribal peoples are lucky enough to have a windfall from a casino operation. So it gives us a chance to be thankful, particularly the day after, when we usually have a nice sunrise ceremony. We speak our piece and share what we've learned. "Here I am on an island with all native peoples." I so appreciate that because it's not only us that paddle but also the elders and people who share their stories, their songs, in the days prior. It strengthens cultural identity.

Pow Wows and Pan-Indian Solidarity

The Annual Chumash Intertribal Pow Wow is an excellent example of how the casino revenues enhance solidarity with other native groups beyond California. Pow wows are not native to California Indians but rather to the plains Indians. However, a pow wow circuit all over the United States has developed over time as a forum for intertribal solidarity and the display of native pride. In the late '60s and early '70s, the tribe hosted small pow wows on the lower reservation, but these operations were modest in size. Today, the pow wow hosts dancers from many tribes, and there are dozens of booths, prize money for the best dancers, several food vendors, and hundreds of visitors. Many non-natives visit to observe the dances, eat fry bread, and visit the vendors' stalls, which ply woven baskets, pottery, jewelry, brightly colored blankets, and many other American Indian arts and crafts.

Bringing native dancers, drummers, and vendors from across the state and the nation, the Chumash are regarded as wonderful hosts by the visitors with whom I have spoken. Decked out in beautiful regalia, dancers compete within different gender and age categories. On the second day there is the grand entry, when all dancers of the various tribes enter the arena together. There is also a public appreciation of individuals who have helped the Chumash over the years.

Besides bringing Indianness into the annual ritual calendar of the valley, the pow wow also fosters intertribal solidarity and educates the larger non-native population of the valley. As Adelina says, "You got Navajo Indians, Indians from Arizona, New Mexico, from the East; this is important for

Indian culture, bringing everyone together. They come and they dance. All these Indian cultures entwined together make a beautiful rug. And even people who went to the mission, to Santa Ynez Days, they also come. It has an impact."

It most definitely has an impact on the Santa Ynez Chumash, who are not only hosts but participants in the dancing. From small children and teenagers to adults and elders, more and more Chumash participate in the dances each year. They make their own regalia and practice the dances for weeks before the pow wow. It has a strong effect on Chumash cultural revitalization in this regard. Just as powerful is the validation that comes from the Chumash watching their dances and prayers in their own language find a place in a large Native American forum. Willie Wyatt speaks to this, explaining, "I think the reason I am drawn to it is that if helps strengthen my tribal identity. Along with that, I think it is important to teach my kids about their Chumash ancestors, what they've gone through and the progress we've made."

The Chumash are promoting intertribal solidarity in other ways. The spiritual leader of the tribe, Adelina Alva-Padilla, has been instrumental in this endeavor, in her capacity as ambassador of her people at other tribal gatherings, and in hosting the Peace and Dignity Runners (members from tribal nations from throughout the Americas who run from Alaska to Panama) at the reservation every year since 1993. Using several thousand dollars of her own funds, Adelina also helped sponsor the 2004 visit of Nobel Laureate Rigoberta Menchu to the reservation. In the Tribal Hall, Menchu was received by the chairman and tribal members as well as by representatives from other Chumash tribes. Chairman Armenta was moved to tears when he met Ms. Menchu, saying, "I don't believe I've ever been caught speechless. I had a feeling I've never had before." The valley has had little experience hosting Nobel laureates, and the articles in the valley and Santa Barbara newspapers show that tribal initiatives are bringing the politics of Indian identity into the local news where they did not exist before.

Passing the Torch: Camp Kalawashaq

In the different instances and levels of cultural revitalization that we have looked at, there is a concerted effort to forge bonds among the generations. This is nowhere so clear as in Camp Kalawashaq, the summer program for Chumash youth.

The summer program was created by the Education Department in 2003. From the beginning, the goal was to provide youth with an appreciation of their cultural heritage and patrimony. With the support and goodwill of Adelina and several other elders and tribal members, the camp grew from ten students the first year to over thirty-five the third. It has continued to grow each year. When it started, the kids ranged from seven to twelve years old, and the interns and youth leaders, also Chumash descendants, were between sixteen and twenty-three. Fieldtrips to painted caves, old village sites, coastal tidal pools, Santa Cruz Island, Vandenberg Air Force Base, Lake Cachuma, and Zaca Lake deepened the children's knowledge of their ancestral homeland and its sacred geography. Rock painting and building an 'ap, or tule reed house, and a full-sized tule reed boat were some of the cultural activities the children engaged in. Local institutions, such as Midland School, UC Santa Barbara, and the Museum of Natural History, hosted the Chumash kids, and anthropologists also cooperated with the program, giving kids a hands-on appreciation of Chumash material culture, history, and plant knowledge. Talking circles and prayers began each day.

After the first year, the scope of the camp expanded to include recreation, storytelling, and native artists. With the hiring of Kathleen Conti— an expert on Chumash history and culture who is currently the director of museum programs, research, and resources for the tribe—the children also made regalia, clapper sticks, deer-hoof rattles, and cradleboards, among other things.

By 2007, Camp Kalawashaq had grown to over forty-five students and had changed in important ways. By that time the camp had become entirely native-run and directed by Nakia Zavalla, the cultural programs director. Almost all adults helping in the day-to-day operation of the camp are Chumash, and the emphasis is on culture. Although there were regalia-making, songs, dance, and native games before, having the Chumash themselves model this behavior makes for a completely engaging experience for the kids.

Camp director Nakia Zavalla makes it clear that cultural knowledge is intimately linked to identify and self-respect.

We have kids that have identity issues with modern-day culture, you know, hip hop, rodeo and cowboy, or whichever. That's fine, but they should always be able to come back to their roots and know who they are. Because when the children don't know their culture, that's when they get lost. Even adults get lost and get involved with things that are destructive to themselves and their bodies or to other people. In the summer program we do prayer in the morning, give thanks, burn sage. It teaches us to walk in a humble way. It teaches the children to be responsible for their actions. We are teaching them life-long lessons, to be honest, to forgive, to always have hope, because those are the things that are easy to lose. For example, we have one of our traditionalists teaching regalia but it's not about just sewing your regalia together, putting the abalone or the beads on the regalia. It's the meaning of it, and how to respect it because if you don't have that, then what does it mean? So we're really teaching them how to take care of it, to pray over it before you put it on, and about protocol—when you should wear it and when you shouldn't wear it.

Nakia says that having Chumash adults run the camp makes kids respectful because everyone knows one another. Most children monitor themselves and there is peer pressure to be respectful of Chumash tradition. "They'll say, 'Come on, we're not supposed to do that, shhh...they're praying—that sort of thing. It's really cool. They are taking the initiative to stop something from happening." And if a problem arises with a child, "we don't do what a normal camp would do—you know, send home a letter. We deal with the kids aside, burn some sage, sit down and talk to them. We want to hear what they want to say. But most of all we have to thank creator and to have him guide us and help us through this problem."

The fact that all the youth leaders are Chumash helps in revitalizing Chumash culture in several ways. Kathy Marshall tells me,

We need to hire the Chumash kids for many reasons. Even though they are older, a lot of them do not know about their culture. A lot of them don't own a *wansaq'*. A lot of them don't have their own regalia. And so this is not just teaching our youth, it's teaching our interns as well. How do we respect our elders, how do we respect our community, how do we respect ourselves? That's really a big part of being a Chumash person, so we're trying to instill it at a young age and teach it to the older youth as well.

The different cultural programs and projects reviewed here demonstrate that cultural revitalization is happening at several levels, from pan-Chumash rituals to the recovery of the Samala language to the cultural education of Chumash youth at Camp Kalawashaq. Yet there are still many other ways that the tribe is gaining cultural power.

The Samala/English Dictionary, published by the tribe in 2007, is a powerful tool for linguistic and cultural revitalization. This was made possible by the remarkable collaboration between Maria Solares and anthropologist J. P. Harrington (1884–1961). Solares spoke fluent Samala and Harrington's lengthy interviews with her were studied by linguist Richard Applegate several decades later. In 2003, Applegate was hired by the tribe to start a language program. Over six hundred pages in length, the Samala/English dictionary is used to recover and teach linguistic, historical, and cultural information. Photo by Gary Robinson.

Maria Solares (1842–1923) was groomed as a culture bearer by her great-uncle and played a decisive role in the preservation of Chumash language and culture. Photo courtesy of the Harrington Papers, National Anthropological Archives, Smithsonian Institution 91-31430.

Maria: An Original Play Honoring the Life of Maria Solares was presented to the public at the Santa Barbara Museum of Natural History in 2012. Honoring a beloved "grandmother" and venerable ancestor hero, the play represents an important shift in cultural awareness and power for the Chumash. Here actors play the parts of Maria and anthropologist J.P. Harrington. Photo by Gary Robinson.

The cast of the play, *Maria.* Photo by Gary Robinson.

William Wyatt and children at the Annual Chumash Intertribal Pow Wow. Bringing "Indianness" into the ritual calendar of the Santa Ynez Valley, the pow wow educates the non-native population and also fosters intertribal solidarity. Photo courtesy of William Wyatt.

Guadalupe Cultural Arts and Education Center, established by Joe Talaugon, has dioramas about local history from a Chumash point of view. Photo courtesy of Joe Talaugon.

127

Chumash children in regalia, proud of their heritage. Photo courtesy of William Wyatt.

Avalyn Grace Wyatt, Chumash descendant. She and other Chumash youth have a bright future, thanks in large part to the casino revenues. Photo courtesy of William Wyatt.

Seven

Cultural Power

"People wonder why we're doing something like that. I've had my own people tell me, 'What you want to do that for? That's the past.' But I say, 'Yeah, that's the past, but do you know what happened to your grandmother, your great-grandma? Do you know that every child, every Indian that died or was killed, they didn't have a chance to reproduce the family? We would have more descendants today and a stronger culture.' You know, there are a lot of missions in California. All these missions were built on the blood and the bones of Indian people, but the majority of people don't know that. They go to the mission, 'What a beautiful place!' But what really happened? What really happened? There was brutality, forced conversion behind all of it. I have enough experience to do something to try to make that change, and if it takes a diorama or the writing of a document to start that change, well, I'm going to do it."

Joe Talaugon, Chumash elder and founder of
Guadalupe Cultural Arts and Education Center

Building on the work of the traditionalists from the late 1960s, it is clear the casino revenues have given Chumash cultural renaissance a strong economic base from which to grow. Among other things, the tribe has been able to hire people with great historical and cultural knowledge to head its museum, culture, and language programs. Besides being used by the tribal government and individuals to revitalize cultural practices and initiate completely new ones, the revenues have provided other forms of cultural power. With its newfound economic and political might, the Chumash tribe is now gaining greater control over its cultural patrimony and over its relationships with government agencies, universities, and museums. The tribe is also rewriting history and challenging the cultural politics of the valley.

Controlling and Repatriating Native Sites and Material Culture

The Chumash use the phrase "government-to-government" to refer to the relationships that the tribal government has with different public agencies, including the US Forest Service, the National Park Service, State Parks, the Channel Islands Park Service, Vandenberg Air Force Base, the county, local municipalities, planning commissions, cities, and state agencies such as Caltrans. Much of the tribe's newfound power has to do with the growth of the tribal government itself. In the past, before the casino, the tribal administrative staff was comprised of just a few people. These individuals were responsible not only for tribal operations but also for getting funds for areas such as education, culture, health, and fire prevention.

Today, there are separate and well-staffed departments in each area. As Willie Wyatt puts it, "As the tribe rapidly progressed, financially and in self-governance, departments were expanded through new programs and services." The creation of a Cultural Programs Department, as well as a Museum Programs, Research, and Resources Department, has also been instrumental in enhancing cultural power. The expansion of the archeological monitoring program and the creation of a cultural preservation consultant position have done the same. In similar fashion, the Elders Committee has gained strength and money for preserving and repatriating Chumash cultural patrimony and for enhancing cultural self-knowledge. Taken together, these different offices within the tribal government indicate the strength of the Chumash's desire to control their heritage and patrimony.

The elders have many responsibilities relating to culture, and one of them is the responsibility of protecting and preserving cultural resources. They deal with many different agencies to oversee Chumash burial sites, village sites, camp sites, and traditional cultural property sites, which include shrines and other sacred sites. As Freddy Romero, the cultural preservation consultant for the elders, says, "Most people don't understand that when you go into an area, it's not necessarily what you see on the ground. It's how we Native Americans perceive that area. You may see trees; we may see a site for prayer or ceremony, and we look to protect these traditional cultural property sites and keep them safe."

The tribal monitoring of archeological digs and construction projects began in the 1970s with the help of Larry Spanne, an archeologist employed by Vandenberg Air Force Base. Many Chumash consider him an important collaborator and friend of the tribe when it comes to cultural resources. As Willie Wyatt says,

> He required that the Air Force consult with the tribe before they approved a project or before they broke ground on a project, and he felt it was important that there was Native American representation on the job when there was the potential of impacting or uncovering artifacts. He has always been there for the tribe. He was a big part of developing the government-to-government consultation model. He made a point to meet every year with the tribe and see if the tribe had any concerns with the work that was going on. That experience transferred over to the tribe's relationship with the Forest Service.

For his work helping to preserve the tribe's heritage, Spanne was honored by the tribe in 2007. Today the tribe has annual consultation meetings with Vandenberg, the Forest Service, the National Park Service, Caltrans, and other agencies.

Although the monitoring program has been going since the 1970s, the enactment of NAGPRA, the Native American Graves Protection and Repatriation Act, in the early 1990s gave impetus to the program. Other laws since then, especially Senate Bill 18, enacted in 2004, have empowered the Chumash even more. Today there are a good number of monitors (consultant-advisors), almost all of whom are Chumash, who work on development projects. Some of these monitors, such as language apprentices

Carmen Sandoval and Frank Dominguez, are especially well versed in Chumash history and culture. The tribe appointed Freddie Romero as a full-time cultural preservation consultant in 2006 to represent the elders in consultation with government and private agencies.

Freddy studied historic preservation law and has learned the language of archeology. He was commissioned by the elders to represent them. "I was told, 'Freddy, we want you to go listen to these people, write a report, come back and make any recommendations based on what they told you in order to preserve our site, in order to prevent them from destroying that site or any mitigations issues that you feel are necessary.' So that's what I do." Freddy explains that the basic idea, when working with government agencies and others, is to impress upon them that there is a lot of cultural material throughout the county. "We want to keep it in the forefront of their minds so that when people are working out there in these areas they understand. 'You know what? We have to be careful about what we are doing out here because this is a culturally sensitive area to the Chumash people.'"

The goal of the tribe is to leave their historic sites undisturbed. As they monitor and educate public agencies and private developers about culturally sensitive areas, they are careful not reveal too much, such as the location of sacred sites. The need to balance preservation with confidentiality arose during the large Zaca fire of 2007. Areas that had not burned for one hundred years were cleared by the fire, making the area vulnerable. In spite of the forest being closed, pot hunters and others looking for cultural artifacts made their way into the back country. The tribe dispatched a crew to sites that were exposed, and as Willie Wyatt tells me, "Many of those sites were covered up again through vegetation rehabilitation projects. Trails were diverted, covering them with brush and concealing exposed areas. We have a fire crew that can do that kind of work—that's big." Here Willie is referring to the tribe's new fire department, which, in addition to its own fire engine and a five-person engine crew, has a ten-person hand crew. This hand crew, with trained archeological monitors, "can actually do rehab work and can go out and protect some of those sites." The tribe also has Pete Crowheart Zavalla, a Native American traditionalist, as its tribal liaison with the Forest Service.

Mitigation work and the protection of Chumash sites and cultural material are not restricted to public lands. The increased power of the Chumash means that they can confront private developers as well. Senate Bill 18 gave added punch to NAGPRA, and now the tribe gets to consult with developers, the City Planning Department, and the county on building projects. "So it gives us an opening to talk to these officials whereas before we didn't—they could just do anything they want. That's why, prior to NAGPRA, so many people and museums got artifacts," says Joe Talaugon, former chair of the Elders Committee. Even after NAGPRA, and until recently, the tribe was not equipped to enforce the law. Freddy says, "We didn't have the understanding as far as education and historic preservation law. How does it affect Native Americans? What rights does it give us? We didn't know that because nobody really shared it. It was just on the books." Today, Joe tells me that the tribe can advise developers, "It's known that there's a village site there, so you either have to go around it or take precautions to deal with it." Although the elders are funded on a yearly basis to maintain and manage the monitoring program, the developer or contractor also has to include the cost of a monitor in the construction bid. This process is now accepted as part of any development project.

Joe says, "It's not enough, but it's a start. Those private land owners don't care. They're not going to call us and say, 'Hey, we discovered some bones over here. Come on out.' No, we have to be on top of it. We don't want human remains disturbed. Now if a burial ground is uncovered, then what should happen is if we can't rebury it right there immediately, then we take those bones and rebury them somewhere else where they won't be disturbed."

Even with their increased power, the Chumash are limited. The tribe can litigate and cause the other party to spend money, but they cannot stop the people from developing certain sites. Freddy explains to me,

> We really don't have a real safe zone in stopping anything, preventing anything. We have compensation and mitigation rights that allow us to sit down at a table with these people and say, "This is an alternative; we would like you to look at it." And it's up to them to decide whether they want to look at it. They can say no. And so what happens is we look at our mitigated measures. This usually results in data recovery by an archeologist hired by the project developer (be it county, state, utility agency, or private developer). We have now lost that resource. This is not what we'd like to have done. The archeologist will then excavate this site in order to recover

cultural material. And it goes in a box and on some shelf in some museum or some shelf in some university somewhere. You look at it that way, we're still losing because we lost the resource. Now this non-renewable resource has been lost forever.

This sense of loss pervades many conversations I have had with the Chumash. As Joe, eloquently expressing the tribe's perspective, puts it,

> Over the past seventy-five years, thousands and thousands of human remains have been bagged and tagged and put on shelves in the universities, museums, different places. All of those have been sitting there for years and years, and nothing has been done with them. Tribes have been trying to retrieve and rebury them, but in most cases there's no place to rebury them. We do rebury certain ones. That is a major problem right now... I feel that the federally recognized tribes that have casinos should come together and try to resolve this problem. It's an enormous problem—all over the State of California, Nevada, Washington State, all over the US. Maybe there should be a national cemetery. Let's start pulling those remains off the shelves and get them reburied. We feel that our ancestors, at the time that they died, when they were buried—well, it's like any other funeral, like any other burial. They were put to rest in the earth—that's where they belong, not up on the shelves.

Freddy Romero expresses a sense of loss and thoughts similar to Joe's when talking about the repatriation of material culture from sites that are being developed—for example, on Vandenberg Air Force Base. "Getting things back from Vandenberg, they lose the area but get things back, get back part of who we are. And through our agreement with them, we are able to return them to the ground from where they've come. That's the main thing—we need to protect our identity, we need to protect our culture, our heritage. That's something we lost. We lost that when we dealt with the missions, we lost that when we dealt with the Europeans. Because they said," and here Freddy's voice adopts a harsh tone, "'Well, we need to take away your native tongue, we need to take away your art, your religion, your identity, your songs, your dance. So now we're going to put you into this area and we are going to teach you how to speak English, how to write and read, and our history, and then this will become your identity. You will no longer be an indigenous person; you'll be a Native American. What does that mean? It means that you're a person that was here long before we got here but we've Americanized you.'"

Rewriting History, Recovering Identity

The politics of culture concern not just native sites and material culture. Native identity and cultural practices can also get appropriated and redefined by mainstream society in a way that many Chumash dislike. For example, there have been cases of new-age groups organizing sweats and charging people to sweat. Freddy says, "That takes away the whole purpose. In a sweat there's an intimacy with those that are there with you. In that space you are going to share things about yourself and who you are, about what's inside you, and find out things about yourself. And you want to know those people are there because we care about one another." There is, then, a strong need for cultural safeguarding and confidentiality, as well as control of knowledge by the tribe.

This same issue is present in the tribe's ambivalent relationship with museums, universities, governmental agencies, and other institutions over the last two centuries. On the one hand, several anthropologists, historians, and other scholars working at the Santa Barbara Museum of Natural History and at UCSB—not to mention J.P. Harrington and Richard Applegate, whose importance we have seen—have created texts that are invaluable for understanding Chumash history as well as current cultural revitalization projects. In recent years, individuals such as John Johnson, Mike Glassow, Larry Spanne, Jan Timbrook, and the late Phil Walker have also actively worked with and in support of the tribe. On the other hand, there is the much larger history of museums and other institutions and their relationship with the Chumash. As we have seen, the Chumash were generally on the outside and not privy to what was written about them. So, until recently, the knowledge generated, although about the Chumash, was not for them.

That changed a little with the native activism and cultural revitalization movements of the '60s and '70s, but the idea of serious cultural repatriation is recent. Freddy Romero puts it bluntly, "They need to return that stuff." Museums, universities, and other institutions have not always worked in the Chumash's best interests, he says. "Why do they need to keep my ancestors' remains for fifty years? We're talking about reburials, not just human remains but also grave goods that were taken. All that stuff needs to get put back into the ground."

Increasingly, many of these institutions are strongly supporting Chumash cultural identity and cultural projects. For example, the tribe now has its own campsite. Pete Zavalla, the Native American liaison between Forestry and the tribe, was instrumental in putting this in place. Kathy Marshall tells me, "It's a beautiful campsite. There's a village site there, so I think it prevented the Forestry from coming in and using the campsite. Now it's for Chumash only—the elders have been working on it for quite some time now. We have our fire guys out there cleaning it up, and we'll be able to be using it for ceremonies. We plan on putting a men's sweat lodge and a woman's sweat lodge out there. So the relationships are building."

The increase in historical knowledge and cultural power has also led to the tribe's approaching Mission Santa Ynez about an Indian Mass and a memorial. Dolores Cross says, "One thing we want to do is have a memorial at the mission for all of the forgotten ancestors that are buried there in unmarked graves, and we have been trying to get that for a couple of years now, working with the church. That's our way of honoring our ancestors who built that mission, who worked and died in the mission." Similarly, the elders have requested that Freddy take the language apprentices out to Vandenberg—where the Chumash currently have special rights to fish and hunt—and visit village sites. As Kathy Marshall describes it, "We will gather together as our ancestors did and do a little ceremony, sing, burn some sage, and do some praying." Through ceremonials and monuments the Chumash are symbolically and ritually reclaiming their land, and in this way reinforcing native identity in both youth and adults.

Some Chumash individuals are also researching and rewriting history themselves. One of the more interesting cultural projects was initiated and is today controlled by a past chairman of the elders committee, Joe Talaugon, who was born in the 1930s. Joe discovered his Chumash identity late in life. Of mixed Chumash and Filipino descent, he grew up in Guadalupe, near Santa Maria, thinking he was part Mexican, not Chumash. It was not until 1970, when Joe was in his early forties, that he discovered he was part Chumash.

Joe learned that his mother, a descendant of Maria Solares, was born in 1914 and spent her first nine years on the reservation. But in the mid-1920s, she and her mother were involved in a terrible car accident. She broke her back, and her mother, that is, Joe's grandmother, was even more severely injured; just thirty years old, she died.

> In her last dying breath, she made my mother swear that she would never admit that she was an Indian: "As long as you live, don't say you're an Indian." My grandmother had had such a hard life, things were so bad, she didn't want her children to live like that. So she gave my mother a different identity to protect her, ease her life for her. You know, maybe it did in some way, but I don't think so. So my mother never grew up knowing anything about the Chumash. She put it out of her mind. Her father raised her, but in Ventura, and she had no connection to the reservation at all.

Joe grows reflective as he discusses this important transformation in his life. "The Chumash part of me didn't even exist until 1970. Then I started dabbling into it and finding more about it, and coming down to some of the pow wows, and meeting some of the people, and I realized who's who." Thrilled to discover his identity, Joe later enrolled in the tribe. "I traced my ancestors back seven generations, and I know exactly what line I come from. So I can attest to the fact that I am a descendant of the early Chumash." Joe became even more involved with American Indian issues, and, realizing the toll that alcohol has taken on American Indians across the land, he gave up alcohol. "From that point on a lot of things opened up to me, getting involved in spirituality."

Joe founded the Guadalupe Cultural Arts and Education Center in 2003. Representing the different peoples found in Guadalupe, including Filipino, Chumash, Chinese, Japanese, Mexican, and Portuguese, the center hosts visiting artists, youth programs, exhibits, and a resident paleontologist. Although Joe was retired and had a nice nest egg, he doubts he could have opened the center without the casino moneys he receives as a tribal member. "I would not have been able to do it. I probably would be just surviving. But that's why I feel I should use the money to build something, and my daughter will continue it on and it will never go away. It will be a legacy."

Joe informs me about what motivated him and the thinking behind the center:

> My thinking in Chumash history is I've done a lot of studying and research, and what I have learned is that a lot of the truth is not told because of different reasons, political or whatever. And I've found that we lost so much, our language, our culture. Everything was lost during those 1800s, during the mission times and during the conversion to Christianity. That's the reason my mother and her mother said those things ["don't say you're an Indian"], because of what happened to their ancestors during the gold rush. You know, there were horrible things happening. I said, "Something has got to be done." And I believe in telling the truth. So when people ask me, "What do you think about the missions? What do you think about what happened to the Indian people?" well, I tell them. They were raped. They were murdered. They were just abused by these invaders. I call them invaders because I believe that our people, the Chumash people, lived here for thousands of years, at least thirteen thousand that we know. In those years, they created their own culture, their spirituality, everything. They lived as a people of their land. Here comes this invader and he takes everything away. Well, a lot of other factors contributed to the beliefs and the culture going away. The alcoholism, death rate, low birth rates, all those things. And so all those things I learned about just kind of piled up within my mind, within my soul, and I said, "I'm going to try and bring out the truth." And that's what I'm going to do here. These dioramas tell the truth and we're not afraid to put it out there.

Joe's dioramas provide a striking contrast with the dioramas at Mission Santa Ynez and the Santa Barbara Museum of Natural History. The first of Joe's dioramas, below a map of the old village sites, shows the Chumash in their pre-colonial, "natural" state, with dolphins, bears, and coyotes. The second, in the mission period, shows soldiers brutally whipping and executing the Chumash who participated in the 1824 revolt. The last of Joe's dioramas shows a building site, with bulldozers lifting human remains out of the ground.

Changing Cultural Politics

Joe is not the only tribal person who thinks it should be the Chumash themselves representing their history. Both the individually and tribally sponsored revitalization projects are helping reshape the tribe and its self-awareness as a people with a distinct history. Until recently, the great amount of knowledge generated in publications and museum displays about the Chumash received very little input from the Chumash, nor was it easily accessed by them. As Niki Sandoval, who worked as a museum professional for more than fifteen years, puts it,

> There was a time when professional researchers would collect American Indian human remains, sacred and ceremonial objects, as well as cultural knowledge. In the name of science, business, or curiosity, researchers would collect what belonged to Native peoples through purchase, trade, or outright theft. Historically, the public interpretation of American Indian culture, history, and life ways was negotiated primarily through the voices of researchers who studied them. Now, Native peoples are speaking with authority and agency about their cultures, histories, experiences, and futures. They are working actively as partners with researchers, and, in several cases, acting as researchers themselves.

So, too, until recently, the Chumash occupied little space in public education, except in stereotypical renditions of the supposedly idyllic Spanish mission period. Today, because of the tribe's newfound clout, this is changing. And as in the case of Joe Talaugon, many Chumash individuals are exploring and reshaping their personal and cultural identities, and their projects and practices are challenging and reshaping the cultural politics of the valley and the region.

As seen in chapter three, the Chumash have also generally been absent in festivities, museums, and monuments in the valley. The tribe lies largely outside the way that the valley represents itself to itself and to others through rituals, symbols, museums, history-making, and local publications. This is changing today. While some revitalization projects are strictly for the Chumash (for example, the solstice ceremony and the Maria Solares celebration), others such as the annual intertribal pow wow and the *tomol* crossing are establishing a Chumash presence in the public sphere and in the valley's annual ritual calendar. In addition, for the last several years, the Chumash have celebrated California Indian Day on September 28 with a large march from the Tribal Hall along Highway 246 to the town of Santa Ynez. In October, there is the Chumash Traditional Gathering, which, while intended primarily for the Chumash, gets some attention in the larger community. And in early November, the tribe hosts a special event for Native American Heritage month. All of these events create a larger Chumash presence in the valley. In much the same way, the Chumash flags flying over their diverse enterprises, the official naming of Highway 154 as the "Chumash Highway," and the tribe's sponsorship of a permanent condor exhibit at the Santa Barbara Zoo give a public face to Chumash historical presence and heritage.

Perhaps more than anything else, the proposed museum and cultural center stand the best chance of tipping the cultural politics of the valley in a way that is inclusive of the Chumash. The plans for this center are ambitious, with an outdoor amphitheater and interpretive park to complement the museum and cultural center. The tribe wants to annex 6.9 acres to the reservation through "fee to trust," in which land is removed from the control of local governments and becomes part of reservation land.

This proposal has been strongly opposed by POLO (Preservation of Los Olivos) and other citizens groups. Some of these opponents charge that, if annexed, the land would be used to put in more slot machines. Others, that it would remove the land from local tax rolls. Others simply oppose anything the tribe does. The Chumash are generally stoic about the controversy, with most expressing certainty that the museum and cultural center will eventually get built. Some think, however, that the valley does not want to recognize Chumash heritage and does not want it competing with the dominant themes of the valley's towns and tourist industries. The museum would be a potent new symbol of Chumash culture, history, and self-determination in the making, putting Chumash culture and history on a par with Spanish, Danish, and local ranching cultures within local society and within the large and growing tourist industry. As one elder Chumash explained, "Well, that's going to put our culture where people can see it, back on the map. Because when people come on through, they'll see a culture center; naturally they're going to want to stop."

Other Chumash are outspoken about the need to represent their culture. As one Chumash man in his mid-thirties puts it, "Right now in Santa Ynez, their culture center is the Maverick Saloon, literally. That's kind of like their landmark in a sense. It's been there many, many years, and nobody knew, passing by 246, that there was a reservation here. And now they will have an opportunity to find out what this land was really about many years ago." Adelina tells me, "Many arriving tourists ask, 'Where are all the native cultures?' Now they are going to have a culture center so people will know how this land was before the other people took over." Adelina turns resolute when she says, "This thing will stop. I always say every hundred years this world changes, and sometimes it changes for the better. The culture center will be part of that change because the real story will be told. Not what someone else wrote and said, 'Okay, these were heathen Indians,' you know?"

Joe Talaugon says it is most important that the displays in the museum come from the Chumash themselves. "Because of culture loss, there is sometimes embarrassment or insecurity and a tendency to lean on outsiders. But now we have the books and education," he says. At the same time, and as we saw in the case of Richard Applegate, the tribe is now in a position to hire cultural experts to assist them in their projects. One of the individuals working hard on the proposed cultural center and to redress centuries of cultural alienation is Kathleen Conti, the tribe's director of museum programs, research, and resources. Her previous museum experience and literacy in Chumash history and culture is a tremendous asset to the tribe. As one elder told me, "Money has helped culture because we are able to hire professional people, like for instance, Kathy. More than eighteen years she studied our Chumash culture."

Many Chumash are aware of how the cultural center will affect local cultural politics. As Joe says,

> The cultural center and museum represents or presents what the truth is, who we really are, and where we came from—and there's enough knowledge to provide that. The center will give an understanding of who our ancestors were and what they did, how they lived. You always have to remember the ancestors and ask for the guidance to provide these things. We have enough people there at the reservation that can do that. A cultural center and museum will really help the outside community understand us better.

Tonie Flores states that it will definitely benefit the whole valley. As she puts it,

The Danish have Danish Days, the cowboys and ranchers have Santa Ynez and Los Olivos Days, the Mexicans have the Fiesta at the Mission Santa Ynez. Chumash culture has always been here, it never has left. And by having that museum we will show that we have never left our homeland. They can have their Danish days and a lot of people come. They can have Spanish days. But I think that in the long run they are going to know who the land really belonged to. By showing them that we were here first before the Danes and the Spaniards, the truth will prevail.

She goes on to tell me that it will especially benefit the valley youth; not just the Chumash kids will get a sense of identity. "Even the white kids don't know the valley's history," she says. "It could change a lot of things." Freddy Romero agrees. He thinks it will draw more visitors to the area and teach them what is really here.

Given the fact that it is coming from a Native American perspective, they would get a much greater understanding. Whether it would change the politics of the community, I don't know. I would like to think so. But I don't think it is going to happen now, with the generations that are living at this particular moment. I think it is for the future generations that it is going to change. Because I think that as time goes on and you have Native Americans that are beginning to mix, slowly but surely that mix will begin to dissolve so that there will be generations that won't remember the ugliness. You know, "That bunch of Indians are savages over there and they're not well educated." Where kids will get admits to college along with the other kids, our economy will allow them to buy in the neighborhoods where they could never buy before and become neighbors with people we have never been neighbors with before because we have the money. Our kids will be raised up with those kids and through that, that ugliness, when it's talked about with kids, who are pretty impressionable, they'll be able to say, "You know what? My friend is Native American and he's not like that." So as time goes on and they raise *their* children, they'll be more open. "You know what? I've heard stories like that about the Chumash, but I know this guy, he's not like that. I can't believe that everybody's like that." And hopefully that will begin to change. Having a cultural center there will begin to reshape things.

The casino revenues, then, are necessary but not sufficient to gain cultural power. Freddy states, "The money has allowed us to focus on these things. Before, we were worried about sustaining ourselves day to day." Today, the Santa Ynez Chumash have greater power to control and promote their heritage, in part through their increased understanding of the law, especially the laws of the last few years that have given them more power over their culture.

We as a people are beginning to read those laws and have interaction with other tribes that have dealt with those laws. A lot of what I am learning in this role is from people who've been on the battlefield already, and about the perspective I need to have when I step into that arena. Money changes everything. Money is power. It gives people the power to go out and buy the attorneys, go out and get educated. But the money is not making us who we are. The money isn't making us Indian. We've always been Indian. We've always been indigenous people. The money has allowed us to go out and be more outspoken about it and promote us more. Whereas before it was just people like my uncle Tony spending money out of his own pocket. I remember he'd go places where he'd have to go and speak and we'd take tents and sleep out of his car because he didn't have money to go buy a room at a hotel. But it allowed us to go out and teach people about who we are. Now with the revenue, we can go out and do many more things.

In sum, the casino revenues have allowed the tribe to hire its own anthropologists, historians, and linguists to recover culture and educate its people. It gives the tribe more power over how the Chumash are understood and represented in local history-making and civic events. And it gives the tribe leverage and negotiating power with museums, universities, private developers, and government agencies over its cultural patrimony and heritage.

Part III

Working Toward Understanding
and Reconciliation

Eight

Critique and Rebuttal

"What it all boils down to, in my opinion, is the fact that a real historical adjustment has yet to take place in the perception of a large portion of the population toward Native Americans. For many people, Native Americans are still perceived as victims—and in their minds, victims aren't supposed to be successful in their entrepreneurial ventures. It wasn't supposed to be in the cards, so to speak, for us to take a scrappy piece of land, build a casino on it, and become one of the valley's largest employers. We were supposed to be frozen in time—forever on a dusty reservation scratching out a living doing odd jobs or perhaps selling blankets on the side of the road. Our ancestors refused to be victims and so do we."

Richard Gomez, vice chairman of the Santa Ynez Chumash

Building on the history and politics reviewed in part one, the second part of this book illuminated the many advances in Chumash education and cultural power during recent years. These advances, as well as the jobs, health clinic, and charitable contributions provided by the casino, benefit not just the Chumash but the larger community. Yet, in spite of these contributions, the tribe continues to be the object of scorn and vociferous attack by certain groups in the valley.

149

My concern here is how these groups' critiques—and the stereotypes and misinformation these critiques often promote—affect the way that Chumash people are regarded in the community, the treatment of Chumash youth in schools, and the way that children of all ethnic groups in the valley grow up thinking about cultural difference. Let us now return to the cultural politics and debates about the Chumash reviewed in chapter three.

Opposition and Misinformation

Those who lead the opposition to the Chumash are for the most part wealthy local citizens, including ranchers and well-known celebrities. A few of these individuals are from the political left but most are from the right. They lead the Concerned Citizens Group, POLO (Preservation of Los Olivos), POSY (Preservation of Santa Ynez), and the local weekly newspaper *The Valley Journal*; some local politicians have also mobilized opposition to the Chumash. While they do raise valid and important issues, these opposition groups also perpetuate a lot of misinformation and misunderstanding.

This is exemplified by the writings of the most outspoken of the celebrity critics, "progressive rocker" David Crosby. Crosby, who even testified in Congress about the casino, has written an autobiography, *Since Then*, in which he devotes a whole chapter to the Chumash. While Crosby has mellowed in his critique of the tribe since he wrote this book in 2006, it is the argument from the book that is discussed below because it reveals and embodies many of the wrong-headed assumptions and stereotypes propagated by the tribe's opponents. Let us now take a critical look at some of these misconceptions, which are also found in articles, editorials and letters to the editor, and even advertisements, in local papers such as the *Santa Ynez Valley News*, the *Santa Ynez Valley Journal*, and the *Santa Barbara News Press*.

Critics of the Chumash Are Equal Opportunity Development Bashers

According to local writer William Etling in a column in the *Santa Ynez Valley News*, the Chumash conflict has to be viewed in the context of opposition to development in general. "The hot button has never been who's doing the developing. It's development itself. There's a heartfelt, sincere, passionate, widespread conviction here that this is a special place, and deserves special care. The quality of life we all enjoy is a direct result." He continues, "A resident since 1966, I'm hard pressed to remember any development plan that wasn't opposed by somebody. Local preservationists are equal opportunity developer bashers."

But, in fact, the Chumash are treated differently. Although opposition groups do oppose other development initiatives in the valley, their attacks on the tribe are often of a different nature and often have an ugly tone not found in their opposition to other projects. There are other contradictions. For example, POLO, one of the most vocal critics of the tribe, has consistently opposed the tribe gaining liquor licenses, expressing great concern about the possibility of increased traffic accidents if the casino allows alcohol. Yet POLO supports the unlimited expansion of wine-tasting rooms, of which there are dozens and dozens in small towns and along rural roadways in the area, because they are "good for agriculture."

Another example of the double standard applied by the most aggressive adversaries of the Chumash is found in the debate over old Matteis Tavern in Los Olivos. Matteis was built in the 1880s, around the time the railroad arrived there. After the mission, it is the largest existing historic structure from that time. Amazingly, Matteis was not recognized as a historical landmark until 2010. Leading up to that was a protracted battle between the new owner of Matteis and a local group over whether the tavern should be declared a historical landmark. The developers opposed this and the subsequent restrictions it would put on them. The response by the standard bearer for preserving Los Olivos, POLO, was surprising. POLO opposed landmark recognition because, it asserted, virtually any property could then be nominated by non-owners for historic land marking status and thus interfere with the owner's use of their private property. As one exasperated letter from a local resident put it, "In that case, I think that they, POLO, should change their name to something other than Preservation of Los Olivos."

The Chumash Are Not "Authentic" Indians

Serious misunderstandings are perpetuated when the tribe is accused of being inauthentic, not "real" Indians. Sometimes their supposed lack of authenticity is based on the claim that they do not adhere to the stereotypical view of natives as being in touch with nature and therefor opposed to development. Another is that tribal initiatives to secure their cultural patrimony and heritage in the region are really just a front, a way to advertise the casino and enhance the tribe's business operation. This charge has been made, for example, in reference both to the proposed Cultural Center and Museum, allegedly a front for more slots, and to the renaming of the Highway 154 as the "Chumash Highway," supposedly just casino advertising.

The most egregious misrepresentation and misinformation about the Chumash occur when their critics challenge the lineage of individual members or of the tribe as a whole. This allegation has been made repeatedly in the local press by the opposition, and, in 2007, it was the subject of a DVD sent out to local residents.

Pseudo experts or "historical consultants" have been hired to look into the tribe's genealogies. For example, an article in 2007 in the *Valley Journal* by one of these "experts" attacked the tribe's authenticity through a selective reading of old census data. The article ignores the tremendous historical documentation surrounding Maria Solares, who, as we have seen, is a culture hero and central figure in the tribe's history and in its cultural revitalization. The author comes to the remarkable conclusion that the name Solares is not linked to the pre-1900 Santa Ynez Indian population. However, any cursory look at books about the Chumash shows Maria's father-in-law, Rafael Solares, in full regalia in the late 1800s—he was chief of the tribe at the time. Five years later, this same "historical consultant" published an article in *Valley News,* again stating that Maria Solares "was not Chumash and was not a member of the Santa Ynez."

A week later, John Johnson, curator of anthropology at the Santa Barbara Museum of Natural History, set the record straight, citing documents that show that Maria and her children, as well as her parents, grandparents, and great-grandparents, were all baptized at Mission Santa Ynez, and that Maria lived her entire life in the valley. Directly attacking the underlying issue, the article ends with, "there is no question but that tribal members today have clear genealogical descent from their ancestors who were part of the original Mission Santa Inés community." Clearly, then, the nasty attacks of the tribe's opponents on their ancestors and heritage involve misinformation, selective data picking, and a distortion of the historical record.

Not just scholars but local residents have also responded to the opposition's attacks on Chumash identity. One commentary in a local paper was extremely eloquent. The author writes that "the consistent claim that any tribe cannot be 'real Indians' because they happen to make someone angry is beating a horse so long dead that it has been fossilized. Of course the members of the Santa Ynez band are 'real Indians'! They have the genealogies to prove it and have been recognized as such by the federal government for over 100 years. The argument over their blood quantum is moot at this point to anyone except themselves."

The author recommends that the critics of the Chumash travel to Ireland. "Tell the Irish that you don't believe they are 'really Irish' because they also have Scandinavian, English, and who-knows-what-else blood. Criticize them because they have 'lost so much of their culture' under oppression. Then let them know you don't approve of the way they decide who is a citizen of their nation. I can only hope that someone will follow with a camera so we can enjoy the reaction on YouTube." The author ends by saying, "Seen in this light, the Santa Ynez band has shown enormous patience and tolerance with people who disrespect them on their own turf."

Casino Tribes Are Bad Neighbors

David Crosby in *Since Then* says, "Ask the people who live around any casino they'll tell you they're bad neighbors. They're not working for the casinos. Everybody, anywhere near any casino, thinks they're shit." Try telling this to the hundreds of locals employed by the casino and the tribe or to the locals who flock to see their favorite country performers, rock bands, and comedy acts. It has been reported that even some of the tribe's harshest critics attend local performances incognito. The local Mexican and Latino population also benefits from having a venue where high profile artists from Latin America and Spain perform.

The tribe has been an excellent neighbor to the low-income people of the valley and larger region who come from as far as San Luis Obispo and Ventura to use the tribal clinic. Similarly, its many contributions and donations to local charities and institutions show that it is sincere in giving back to the community. The tribe has also managed its operation from a "green" perspective. The Tribal Hall and the Tribal Clinic are run on solar power, and the tribe has won environmental awards for the casino operation itself. One source notes that in this regard, "the Chumash efforts are not only at the forefront of what anyone else is doing in Santa Barbara County; they appear to be leading the state in this sort of development."

The Chumash also give a lot back to their community through their Santa Ynez Chumash Foundation and the large fundraisers it sponsors. Not surprisingly, the Chumash donate a lot to the social service organizations that used to help them when they were poor. For example, several people from the tribe donated their time to the telethon of the Unity Shoppe of Santa Barbara and the tribe donated seventy-five thousand dollars to the organization, which provides struggling families with food and clothing. The same is true for Toys for Tots, which used to provide needy Chumash children with one new toy for Christmas. And one of the tribe's largest donations was for $3 million to Santa Ynez Union High school, the alma mater of many Chumash.

But Chumash generosity extends far past the organizations that helped them in the past. The list of donations includes a $1-million-dollar donation to the Santa Ynez Valley Cottage Hospital; support for the annual Chumash Golf Classic Tournament, which, in 2008 alone, raised over one hundred thousand dollars for two local charities, People Helping People and the Santa Barbara Foodbank; over one hundred thousand dollars to the local YMCA; and donations to many other organizations, such as Life Chronicles (which video records messages of comfort to individuals with health crises), Arts Outreach (which provides art, music, dance, and theater workshops for students in the valley), and food banks (which provide turkeys at Thanksgiving and food year-round to families in need). In 2009, the Chumash also donated twenty thousand dollars to the Blackfeet Reservation in Montana for their high school and one hundred thousand dollars for Hurricane Katrina and Hurricane Rita victims. In short, Chumash generosity and support for the community shows that they have in fact been good neighbors.

The Casino Alone Is Responsible for Increased Crime

According to Crosby, casinos "inevitably bring crime to a community." Crosby's point is undeniable. There has been an increase in crime in the valley, and a significant portion of it is clearly due to the casino. In 2009, for example, 154 arrest/offense reports were made at the casino, and these included alcohol- and drug-related crime, theft, forgery, and battery. Petty theft has also substantially increased in the area, with break-ins of cars and homes occurring more often than before.

But crime has also increased greatly in all of northern Santa Barbara County since 2000, especially in nearby Santa Maria and Lompoc, which have gangs. There is a spillover effect from these areas, and this crime is unrelated to the casino. The police blotters in local newspapers report many incidents of domestic disputes, drunk driving, possession of drugs, and the like that are completely unrelated to the casino. There is also the growing population of the valley with its attendant road traffic, which is also increased by traffic heading to wineries and tasting rooms. In sum, while it has certainly contributed, the casino should not be blamed for all the crime and traffic in the valley.

Casino Revenues Do Not Benefit the Local Economy or Community

Crosby asserts that the casinos "say they put money into local economies but the truth is that almost all of it goes out of town, out of state, and offshore." This is not true. The casino benefits the local economy tremendously, and in many different ways. The casino and other Chumash properties, as well as the employees, pump a large amount of money into the local economy. The tribe has purchased other properties locally and has established other businesses. Many of the tribal members themselves and their descendants, capitalized by the casino revenues, have also established businesses locally and contribute through their spending as well.

The tribe employs over fifteen hundred people in its various enterprises, purchases millions of dollars of goods and services from local vendors, and provides a clinic that helps subsidize the health care costs for many businesses, ranches, and households. It also contracts big-name entertainers and provides some of the nicest hotels and restaurants in the region.

A 2008 economic study funded by the Santa Barbara County Tax Payers Association found that from 2001 until 2006 the total annual expenditures of the Chumash casino went from around $95 million to $235 million. The Chumash Resort and Casino was the second-fastest-growing employer in Santa Barbara County and provided "an annual economic stimulus of $336 million (total impact). For every ten jobs created by the casino, there were four additional jobs in the community (indirect impact). These additional jobs produce an additional $30 million in annual payroll dollars (induced impact)." Casino salaries averaged about forty thousand dollars a year for its more than fifteen hundred workers, giving the lie to the critics who say that the casino provides only poor-paying jobs.

The casino also contributes to government tax revenue and to the income of local businesses. The report estimates that the casino operation generated the collection of $16.6 million in state and federal payroll taxes, and over $35 million in state, federal, and local income taxes. The operation spent $185 million on labor, goods, services, and distributions of income in the county. "The respending by Chumash Casino employees is a significant economic driver resulting in $58 million in additional sales and $14 million in tax payments to the government." The casino resulted in the creation of over nine hundred new jobs in the county economy between 2002 and 2008. Concluding that the "facts are difficult to ignore," the report also notes that the different revenues generated by the casino resort fund "essential government programs and services including law enforcement, fire protection, and local and regional road maintenance."

The report finds that the casino brings tourists and visitors from adjacent counties, and they spend their money in a variety of local businesses, not just the casino resort. Indeed, it found that the casino accounted for over 25 percent of out-of-town visitors and had a higher than normal "multiplier effect" for tourist-related businesses, helping reduce a trend of declining tourism.

As we saw above, the Chumash have donated to local organizations of many kinds. All of this giving is in addition to that mandated by various compacts. By 2006, the Chumash had already paid over $13 million into the Special Distribution Fund, which is part of a state-mandated process of distributing tribal casino profits through the Indian Gaming Community Benefit Committee, "to help local governments handle off-reservation impacts of tribal gaming." The committee granted more than $1.4 million in 2007 to the police and fire departments, as well as to other local organizations affected by the casino. It also has its own fire department, which coordinates with the county.

All these contributions and the local economic impact of the Chumash, however, are downplayed and attacked by their opponents. As one critic who wrote a series of anti-Chumash articles in the *Valley Journal* put it, "The creation of a few largely low-paying transient and unprotected jobs, and a few token gifts made periodically over the years to various charities does not come close to off-setting the many serious impacts and economic costs caused by the Chumash casino."

Many locals beg to differ. One letter-writer, responding to this critique of the tribe, says that if you were to look at Chumash contributions, "you would find philanthropy in 'ginormous' proportions! In fact, you would hang your head in shame over ever having doubted the good the Chumash have done for our community! I haven't seen any other organization in the Valley match or come close to giving." She adds, "Why do we try to alienate the one organization that gives generously, in such proportions that it dwarfs any other organization? We are so quick to judge but we aren't looking in the mirror! Do we really have to wait for Mr. Armenta to write out yet another check in order to see improvement? At least he hasn't been distracted with hatred and instead focuses on the positive. We should follow in such a manner."

Indians Insist on Special Rights, Do Not Pay Taxes, and Are Lawless

Implicit in the Chumash opponents' arguments is that American Indians somehow invented and are to be blamed for the concept of native sovereignty, and that they are thus anti-American. Crosby, for example, says, "They can do anything they want and they don't have to play by the same rules as us, and that was the crux of it: this is America, they're Americans, whether they like it or not. They're proud of saying they were the first Americans. Well, they're still Americans. They tell us they're sovereign nations and they're very snotty about it. Bullshit. They're still under the federal government and they're still Americans."

As we saw earlier in this book, the reservation system was foisted on the indigenous people, and because of that colonial policy and acts of Congress, tribal members in federally recognized tribes are today dual citizens—that is, both American citizens and citizens of their own tribe. It is both/and, not either/or. Many American Indians, including most of the Chumash, are extremely patriotic. In fact, a much larger percentage of them have served in the armed forces than among non-natives, and they don't need to be told they are Americans.

Crosby, voicing a common misconception, also states that the Indians "use our schools, roads, hospitals, firemen, and police, and they don't pay taxes." But while American Indians who live and work on an Indian reservation are exempt from paying state income tax, they do pay federal taxes, and the Chumash pay sales taxes just like everybody else. The more than fifteen hundred employees of the tribe have to pay both federal and state taxes. And, as we saw above, the casino has generated tens of millions of dollars in state, federal, and local income taxes.

A topic of much debate in the valley is the "fee-to-trust" process. If the Chumash can add property they purchase to their reservation through this process, they can circumvent zoning agreements and building codes. After the establishment of the casino, a lot of local conflict was centered on the Fess Parker/Chumash proposal for a residential resort on fourteen hundred acres well off the reservation that would be annexed to the tribal land. Because of fierce opposition, the proposal was eventually scuttled by the tribe. However, the tribe is now trying annex that land, as well as the 6.9 acres for their Museum and Cultural Center, through the fee-to-trust process. These initiatives are hotly contested by the usual opponents of the tribe as well as by a large number of other local citizens.

Fee-to-trust could have far-reaching consequences across the nation, and both individuals and local citizen groups have every right to protest fee-to-trust if they want. But the way that the Chumash and Native Americans in general are portrayed in their opponents' critiques is often offensive. For example, Crosby says, "If they get to take any piece of land and make it part of tribal property, then they can build anything they want, anywhere they want. They can build a casino next to a school. They can build a garbage dump next to a school. They can build a nuclear power plant, a slaughter-house, next to a school." Again, Native Americans are portrayed as lawless and as having no regard for the larger community.

The Community Opposes the Tribe

We find "the community" narrowly defined by the critics of the Chumash time and again. Opponents often speak about what "the people" want, asserting that "everyone," "most of the people here," and "the community" are against tribal initiatives. These opponents exaggerate the strength and numbers of their base, and it is clear that their definition of "the community" includes only those white ranchers, celebrities, and upper-middle-class residents who support their cause. Yet there are hundreds and hundreds of Chumash descendants, Latino residents, and whites who support the Chumash and who make up a large percentage of the local population. If we include these individuals, many more of the people living locally support the tribe than oppose it. In sum, and as seen in the case of Matteis Tavern and the debate over wine-tasting rooms, some groups that purport to represent the interest of "the community" in fact represent a much smaller, elite constituency.

Chumash Responses

Although the tribe has shown restraint in responding publicly to much of this criticism, in private many Chumash are bothered by the opposition's attacks. In particular, the practice of questioning their authenticity and identity is seen as a cheap shot and offensive to their ancestors and to who they are as a people. Kathy Marshall tells me,

> I have tried so hard to avoid the papers lately because there is just no truth; the tribal opponents don't get it. The last article I read was in the *Valley Journal*; actually I got a DVD on a meeting that they had, suggesting that we were possibly Shoshone and not Chumash, and that one really hurt my feelings. You can say whatever you want about the casino, but not about our ancestors. A lot of people say, "You can't dwell in the past, we didn't do that to you." But those were our elders, those were our relatives, and we need to always honor what they went through and never forget it. They're making it sound like it was thousands of years ago; you're talking recent, less than a hundred years ago. We will always carry the scars of our ancestors.

Another of the allegations made by the critics is that the Chumash have brought harm to the valley; this is also hotly contested by the Chumash. As Freddy Romero says, "We're just trying to survive, assuring our next generation that we have a financial base." Despite the tribe's newfound wealth and power, he still views the tribe as battling a long-standing power structure. "Here's a people that finally got to a place where they don't have to rely on the government. We don't have to rely on the commodity trucks backing up into the reservation to drop food off for us. We have our own health center; we don't have to go down to a general hospital and wait hours and hours to be seen by a doctor and get mediocre care. We're able to take care of our own people."

Joe Talaugon blames ignorance and jealousy rather than outright prejudice:

> I believe the Chumash Indians lived in the Santa Ynez Valley before the white man came, but because through the years the ways the whites settled in the Santa Ynez Valley, they didn't

even pay attention or even know there was Indians living down the street. So they were nothing. So here all of a sudden out of this creek grows this big casino, a money-making multimillion dollar thing, and they say, "They shouldn't have it. They don't deserve it. They're nothing but stupid old dumb Indians." Well, that proves to me that they're not stupid Indians because someone got educated and somebody knew how to establish a business. And here we are.

Many Chumash are also offended by how their opponents are often anti-immigrant, when the critics themselves—like all Americans, except for American Indians—are of immigrant stock. It bothers the Chumash when they are confused with Mexican immigrants and are subjected to the same treatment. "We still get that thing: 'Well, you can just go back from where you came from.' And it usually comes from somebody of Anglo descent. And we say, 'You know what? We're not the ones who crossed over here in a boat,'" Freddy says laughing.

Indeed, a running joke among many Chumash is that the pilgrims were the first illegal immigrants and the natives should have asked them for their green cards. "What, no green card?" a Chumash friend kids me. "Sorry, can't come in." This same sentiment is expressed on some of their tee shirts that feature glowering American Indians with the logos, "Illegal immigration started in 1492" or "Immigrants threatening your way of life? Must be tough."

All in all, many of the critiques and contradictions of the opposition are just not that important to the Chumash. They feel that the arguments are misdirected and that time will prove the tribe right. Yet they can also be self-critical. As Reggie Pagaling says, referring to the casino and the programs it has spawned, "It has come in leaps and bounds. Sure, we still have the cart before the horse, but we're almost there. When I say cart before the horse, I mean that we make a lot of mistakes as a group with the revenues. At the same time, all that has been an educational process for us." Having the tribe transformed from being on welfare to being an economic powerhouse and leader in the county, Reggie says, is "a total change of identification, of respect. And then there is the process of education—for us, and for those who don't recognize us. That's huge!"

Nine

Moving toward Understanding
and Reconciliation

"This country was built on the idea that we all play from the same rule book, that we're all on the same page, that the essence of America is equality. All men are created equal. Not 'All men are created equal but the Indians get special breaks.'"

David Crosby

"I want to pass along how sick and tired many of us are of hearing all the recent arrivals bashing the Chumash and the casino. They were here long before any of us. The White man was kind enough to confine them to a crummy piece of land in Santa Ynez, and guess what? They have turned it into a gold mine. If that was you or me who had created that kind of business, we would be patting each other on the back."

Letter to the editor, *Santa Ynez Valley News*

This book has provided historical and cultural reporting to understand an important contemporary issue in a particular context, that of the Chumash in the Santa Ynez Valley. It has been about educational marginalization and about the different ways that they lost control over their destiny as a people.

It has also been about their overcoming this sad history and regaining political and cultural power. This until now largely untold story challenges prevailing stereotypes of casinos destroying indigenous culture. Against a historical backdrop of terrible culture loss—through the suppression of language, religion, and identity—we saw that the casino revenues have strengthened a collective revitalization movement begun in the late 1960s by individual families. Now the tribe and its members have the time and resources to make this a united tribal endeavor. From a dearth of educational prospects, the Chumash have created almost unlimited opportunities. So, too, the tribe now has much more leverage and power over its cultural patrimony and heritage.

Yet, as we saw in the last chapter and previously in chapter three, larger cultural politics and misconceptions about American Indians continue to vex the Chumash. In this regard, critics of the tribe condition the local perception of the Chumash and work against a sympathetic understanding of the tribe and its people. At the same time, the tribe's newfound cultural and political power is also challenging and reshaping these cultural politics.

An Alternative View

The preceding chapters suggest an alternative view of history and society in this region of rural California. The standard view, as represented in local civic celebrations, museums, and the public education system, ignores the Chumash and the great cultural diversity that exists in the valley. In addition to ranch culture, Western heritage, and the still vital traditions of the Danes who settled Solvang, the valley is also home to the rich history and cultural life of its resident Latino population as well as the ceremonies and heritage of the Chumash. These, too, deserve celebration and a place in local history.

The education system and popular representations propagate a romantic portrayal of the missions and Spanish colonization, and these developments are seen as taking place in the distant past with no relevance to the present. Although Spanish and Mexican rule over the valley lasted only a half-century, Hispanic heritage has been a constant part of valley life since that time. Many Chumash have a lot in common with local Mexicans, including a shared history, Catholicism, a good deal of intermarriage, and use of the Spanish language. But the Chumash also have a unique culture, forged in an antagonistic social context, and this distinguishes them from whites and Mexicans alike.

Because of the class and racial politics of the valley, it is no surprise that some of the opponents of the Chumash are also very much opposed to Mexican and other Latino immigrants. The Latino ranch and farm workers, who are integral to the agricultural and pastoral enterprises in the valley, bring unique skills in these areas and are proficient at what they do. Yet not only are they the most vulnerable in regard to working conditions and police harassment, but they are accused of being drains on our social institutions. Similarly, the Chumash are represented by their opponents as having no regard for the valley, as inauthentic, and as perpetrators of a "scam." Chumash business enterprises are criticized as being at odds with American Indian heritage and as leading to culture loss. We have seen that none of this is the case.

Although the casino has undeniably had negative impacts, such as increased crime and traffic, it has also had many positive impacts. Contrary to a great deal of negative press that the tribe has received, my alternative view stresses the positive contributions that the Chumash have made both for themselves and for the valley as a whole. They have taken an opportunity that was presented to them and used it to improve their lives and those of many of their neighbors through their health clinic; their assistance to the valley's needy, local schools, and youth organizations; the huge numbers of jobs and services they provide; their spin-off enterprises such as restaurants, hotels, and concert venues; and their contributions to the knowledge and culture of the area.

We have seen the tremendous educational opportunities now available to Chumash, young and old, and how better education is transforming the tribe. We have also seen the increasing role of the tribal government in spurring on collective ritual and the recovery of the Samala language. The tribe now has well developed, formalized departments with a growing staff dedicated to education and culture and to the preservation of Chumash heritage. The tribe is gaining a presence and also educating the larger community about the valley's history and heritage.

Yet in spite of this, as we saw in the last chapter, some opponents demonize the tribe, ignoring the advances it has made and its contributions to the larger community. Clearly, in spite of protestations to the contrary, the Chumash are treated differently from other developers. A whole range of stereotypes and misinformation comes into play, and the attacks made on the tribe often have a mean, personal edge to them. Although some of the issues brought up by the critics are valid, others are not. Their misrepresentations strengthen negative stereotypes of the Chumash, and these filter down to the valley's youth.

Understanding the Past, Healing the Rift

Yet more and more people in the valley are crossing cultural divides and benefiting from the great diversity that exists here. Increasingly, along with region's famous tri-tip barbecue, fabulous wine, Danish *ableskivers*, and Mexican *chiles rellenos*, locals are trying Indian fry bread. Many residents who benefit from the Elverhoj, Hans Christian Anderson, and Carriage House museums are waiting expectantly for the proposed Chumash Museum and Cultural Center to open. So, too, some local schools are teaching children about Chumash and Mexican heritage in the valley, as well as about its Western traditions. More and more people, in addition to attending the Fourth of July and Danish Days processions in Solvang and participating in the celebrations of Santa Ynez Day and Los Olivos Day, now also attend the Annual Chumash Intertribal Pow Wow and watch the Native American heritage procession in Santa Ynez. In sum, more local residents and educators are finding that the valley can be "both/and," rather than "either/or," and that understanding and participating in its diversity is enriching, both culturally and economically.

Reconciliation and understanding can be further advanced if the critics of the tribe acknowledge that, although there is a downside to having a casino in the valley, it has brought many benefits, not just for the Chumash but for the community as a whole. In spite of the often acrimonious discussion between the Chumash and their opponents, amends can be made and a stronger community forged. The valley can teach its children well, drawing on its diversity for strength and fostering cross cultural understanding.

The school system, newspapers and other media, and museums should advance the general public's understanding of the particular history of the Chumash and the valley. There has to be an understanding that Chumash identities have been subordinated to and have melded with those of Spanish, Mexican, and other peoples over the last two hundred years, and that, in spite of this, the Chumash have been able to maintain a distinct identity.

In order to go beyond the stereotypes about American Indians, people also need to learn about the history of native relationships with the state. As dual citizens, American Indians who form part of federally recognized groups such as the Chumash have a different relationship with the state than do other citizens. These federally recognized groups have their own criteria for enrollment, and, while the application of the criteria may not be perfect, it is these groups that control the process. No longer do outsiders have the right to define who is Indian and how Indians should act in the world.

Critics should also stop questioning the ancestry of the Chumash and their efforts to promote Chumash heritage. They should recognize that rather than destroying traditional culture, the casino revenues have supported the cultural revitalization movements started in the late '60s, and that although casino revenues do create tension between recognized and non-recognized tribes, they have also been used to foster cooperation between different Chumash groups and between the Santa Ynez Chumash and other American Indian tribes.

As far as supporting Chumash heritage and the tribe's central role in the history of the valley, the Chumash Museum and Cultural Center, once built, will have a large impact. As Kathy Marshall says,

> Having a Chumash cultural center for the valley will be huge, a great place to be able to educate the people that don't really understand. You know, when we're talking about the new museum, the opposition was saying, "They're going to put slot machines in there!" We honor the artifacts our ancestors made. We all do songs and prayers as we bring these back into our lives. We would never disrespect or dishonor them by putting a slot machine in our museum. We need to be able to reclaim things. Families that have been in this valley for generations have collected some of our artifacts, and I hope they'd come forward and give those things back to us. For us, whether they are in a museum or with a private collector, those artifacts are a piece of us.

Those who oppose Chumash initiatives have every right to do so. But what is counterproductive is the misinformation and misguided personal attacks perpetuated by these groups and the stereotypes that these attacks play on and reinforce. In attempting to heal the rift between the Chumash and their detractors, critics should stop questioning the authenticity of the tribal members.

Another way to help heal the rift is to stop generalizing the behavior of a few "bad eggs" on the reservation to the entire Chumash tribe. Yes, intergenerational trauma from the past makes for some difficult cases on the reservation, that is, people who get into drugs and alcohol or who flaunt their wealth. But there are similar behaviors in every ethnic group in the valley. And as seen throughout this book, many Chumash are devoted to their Education Department, Cultural Programs Department, Health Clinic, and other venues for assisting their people and the community.

Critics of the tribe should also stop misinforming people that the casino revenues benefit only the one hundred and fifty or so tribal members. We have seen that the per capita payouts help their large extended families and that more than twelve hundred descendants can now take advantage of the vast educational opportunities that the tribe provides. By the same token, critics of the tribe should acknowledge that the tribe has been generous with the surrounding community, that it has diversified its enterprises, and that the valley as a whole gains from the fine dining and world-class entertainment they provide.

Another way to heal the rift between the past and the present and between the different groups in the valley would be for some of the large ranches in the area to allow the Chumash access to their ancient village sites. The Chumash in fact have permission from one large landholding to visit and do ceremony at a major village site, and they are extremely respectful and appreciative of that opportunity. Such actions would foster good will and mutual respect.

As far as bridging differences with regard to education, Chumash Education Director Niki Sandoval emphasizes that this can best be achieved through collaboration among tribal people, educational researchers, parents, and educators in the valley. Prior to this collaborative work, however, "all participants must acknowledge the emotional and difficult history of the relationship between schools and Native community members in the local area... It is important for teachers to hear the stories of Native community members in order to begin to understand the people they serve."

Perhaps on the other side of the rift between the Santa Ynez Chumash and the wider community, the tribe can work to further mitigate and contain the negative impacts of the casino on the valley. Maybe they can also set aside more funds to help other Chumash and native California groups above and beyond the two funds that they already pay into. Along the same lines, perhaps the Chumash can develop "sister reservation" relationships with other indigenous communities in countries such as Mexico and Peru, where a little bit of money goes an extremely long way.

The Santa Ynez Chumash tribe is just one native community among thousands and thousands throughout the Americas. The overwhelming majority of the more than 45 million indigenous people who live in these communities continue to suffer the consequences of hundreds of years of colonization and political, economic, and educational marginalization. Perhaps the Chumash and other tribes with casinos will lead the way to securing a better future not only for themselves and their future generations, but also for less fortunate native groups within the United States and elsewhere. In this regard, perhaps the future Chumash museum and cultural center will be a place that promotes cooperation with indigenous peoples throughout the Americas.

Finally, it is my hope that this book encourages others, Chumash and non-Chumash alike, to look deeper into the historical and cultural forces that surround us. While the experience of each of the other casino tribes and their surrounding communities, in rural California and elsewhere, has to be understood in its particular context, the perspective presented here can be broadened to these other tribes and their impacts. In looking at the interplay between different ethnic groups in these contexts, we must ask: Which cultures are recognized as authentic and legitimate and enshrined in history, school texts, and civic celebrations? Which are not? Why not? How is this changing? Clearly, the accomplishments of tribes such as the Santa Ynez Chumash figure importantly in this changing reality.

Endnotes

Preface

The epigram by Darian-Smith that preceded the preface was taken from Darian-Smith (2004:xi). That of Adelina Alva-Padilla is from an interview conducted by the author. That by C. Cordero is from *SYVJ* (August 6–12, 2009:15). As for the use of the word "renaissance" in the title, I refer the reader to the incisive words of a prominent anthropologist, Marshall Sahlins, regarding the reinvention of tradition. "For it happens that in the 15th and 16th centuries a bunch of indigenous intellectuals and artists in Europe got together and began inventing their traditions and themselves by attempting to revive the learning of an ancient culture which they claimed to be the achievement of their ancestors but which they did not fully understand, as for many centuries this culture had been lost and its language (Greek and Latin) had been corrupted or forgotten.... All this came to be called the Renaissance in European history, because it gave birth to 'modern civilization.' What else can one say about it, except that some people have all the historical luck? When Europeans invent their traditions—with the Turks at the gates—it is a genuine cultural rebirth, the beginnings of a progressive future. When other peoples do it, it is a sign of cultural decadence" (Sahlins 2002:4). The title "Chumash Renaissance" was chosen to challenge this idea.

xxiii *College was not much different.* While studying Anthropology and Spanish at Humboldt State University in the late '70s, I did meet a few Indians and "half-Indians" at school, surfing, and while camping in the Trinity Alps. But these were chance encounters with just a few individuals, and to me they were small exceptions that proved the rule: Indians used to be here but now were almost all gone.

Little suggested otherwise. The book I read that reinforced that perception was *Ishi in Two Worlds* (Kroeber 1961). To find out the real scoop about Ishi, the "last survivor of Aboriginal America" (found in northern California in 1911), and about California Indians in general, see Starn 2004. For the massacre of the Wiyot on Indian Island, one of more than 56 such massacres in Humboldt County alone, see Raphael (2007:164-179).

xxiv   *My first exposure to indigenous society was outside of California.* I learned Spanish and Quechua, and after taking my master's degree from a Peruvian University and my doctorate in the US, I taught anthropology at the University of California at Riverside for thirteen years. I specialized in Andean culture and highland Peru, researching and publishing on irrigation, cultural politics, indigenous narratives, and transnational migration (see, for example, Gelles 1990, 1995, 1996, 1998, 2000, 2002, 2005b; Martinez and Gelles 1993, 2013). The deeper I read into Chumash history and cultural politics, the more I find that the Chumash have been subjected to economic and political marginalization, as well as cultural stereotyping, similar to that of Andean and other indigenous peoples in Latin America. In spite of the similarities, however, we need to understand the particularities of Chumash culture and their historical experience.

xxv   *The opportunity to do so arose when I moved my family to the Valley...* In 2005, after gaining permission to pursue research with the tribe, I was commissioned by the Center for California Native Nations (CCNN) at the University of California at Riverside to write a report on the Chumash (Gelles 2005a); CCNN was largely funded by CNIGA (California Nations Indian Gaming Association). Then, in the summers of 2007 and 2008, I received funding from SITG (Sycuan Institute for Tribal Gaming) to carry out more research. In the cases of CNIGA and SITG, the funds come mainly from Pechanga and Kumeyaa tribes, respectively. As far as the research itself, anthropological research is different from that of other disciplines, such as sociology or journalism, in that it is more immersive and based on long-term participant observation, what anthropologist Clifford Geertz calls "deep hanging out" (Geertz 1998). The idea is that, through cooperation and trust, one will gain increased insight into a people and their life ways. My interviews with the Chumash were long and open-ended and were usually conducted after I had known the person for a while. We discussed many topics, including education, culture, discrimination, tribal power, life on "the Rez," and local valley politics. The material for this book also comes from my participant observation since 2003, teaching in the summer program and attending many cultural events, such as pow wows, Ramada Gatherings, Bear Ceremonies, the visit by Nobel Laureate Rigoberta Menchu, Christmas celebrations, graduation ceremonies, and the tribe's launch of the Chumash dictionary. In addition to long interviews and participant observation, I analyzed newspaper clippings that document various political and cultural issues involving the tribe. As a Spanish speaker, I also have access to local Latino views and their experience of life in the valley, including their relationships with the Chumash.

xxv   *At the same time, working for the tribe has turned my experience as an anthropologist on its head...* Anthropology, as a discipline, used to be the handmaiden of European colonialism, helping the colonial powers and newfound nation-states oversee, understand, and control their subject peoples, be these in far-flung colonies or inside the home countries of the colonists. In the Americas, it developed largely as a way to understand, contain, and control the native populations while consolidating control over their territories. In the 1970s, anthropology changed radically. Before that time, it was very rarely put at the service of the "objects of study," the indigenous peoples themselves. For example, Chumash cultural artifacts collected by archeologists and grave robbers are found in museums around the world. Similarly, while much ink has been spilt by anthropologists and historians on this people—the Chumash are the most well documented of California Indian tribes—this material, until recently, was rarely made available to, or served the needs of, the Chumash themselves. This is now changing.

Introduction   Chumash Empowerment and the Politics of Culture

p. 3   *Although supported by many local residents, the Chumash have faced and still face stiff opposition from others.* Eve Darian-Smith's incisive study, *New Capitalists: Law, Politics, and Identity Surrounding Casino Gaming on Native American Land* (2004), studied the politics surrounding the construction of the casino in Santa Ynez, especially the use of stereotypes by those who were opposed to it. As she says, the new found political, legal, and social power of some casino tribes has challenged "in profound ways the manner in which many non-Indians define North American citizens, society, and processes of capitalism" (Eve Darian-Smith, 2004:xi).

p. 4   *My perspective on the Chumash is rooted in the larger context of the problems and prospects facing indigenous groups throughout the Americas.* The United Nations definition is taken from Van Cott (1994: 23).

p. 5   *Yet, despite their large numbers and the large territories indigenous people control...* The images and racism that feed into the discrimination faced by indigenous people are still fairly pervasive. In Latin America, even in those countries with indigenous cultural majorities (e.g., Guatemala, Peru), indigenous people are grotesquely parodied on television shows and in the national press. In the United States, despite certain established rights and empowerment over the last few decades, images of native peoples are still used to sell cars and as sports mascots. And, in Canada, the construction of the nation-state is largely seen as only concerned with the cultural rights of French and English speakers, excluding those of indigenous peoples. In more extreme cases—such as in Peru, Guatemala, and Brazil—massacres like that which happened to the Wiyot tribe in Northern California in the nineteenth century were still happening in the late twentieth century. And although there are exceptions—the Zuni tribe of New Mexico, the Otavalo people of Ecuador, and indigenous transmigrants to the United States from communities in Mexico, Central America, and the Andean region come to mind—most Indians are poor and still experiencing the effects of colonialism and marginalization. Throughout the Americas, indigenous cultural identities are inextricably linked—by representations in popular culture, nationalist doctrine, and even scholarship—to images of poverty and marginalization, the implicit message being that to achieve social mobility, indigenous peoples must renounce their identities. Yet indigenous people from Peru to Canada increasingly transit urban and national boundaries, adopting new technologies and prospering without sacrificing their identities. In sum, the cultural distinctiveness of indigenous peoples is compatible with modernity and social mobility. This is the case with the Chumash.

p. 5   *The relationship of the United States government with its indigenous people...* For an excellent discussion of sovereignty, I highly recommend Gary Robinson's film *Tribal Sovereignty. The Right to Self-Rule* (2007), which also addresses many myths regarding casino tribes and the purpose of the revenues they generate. See also Spilde (2003) for the ways in which casino tribes provide benefits to California. And for other discussions of casinos, cultural identity, and sovereignty, see, among many others, Cramer 2005, Cattelina 2008, Robbins 2011, Spilde 2004, 2006, Gardner, Kalt, and Spilde 2005, Spilde, Taylor, and Grant 2006.

One   Early Chumash History and the Creation of White Culture in the Santa Ynez Valley

The epigram is taken from Miller (1988:37).

p. 13   *To understand why education and cultural revitalization are so important to the Santa Ynez Chumash, we must look to history.* The Chumash have been the object of more scholarly publications than any other tribe in California. The historical material for this book, taken largely from secondary sources, is intended to provide background context for understanding the present-day Santa Ynez Chumash. For those wanting a more in-depth look at the cultural history of the Chumash in general, there is a wealth of sources on diverse topics such as history, society, ritual, political organization, astronomy, myths, and stories (see, for example, Applegate 1975a, 1975b, Blackburn 1975, Gamble 2008, Gardner 1965, Haley and Wilcoxon 1997, Holmes and Johnson 1998, Hudson 1979, Hudson et. al 1981; Robinson 2005, 2007, Miller 1988, Johnson 1988, 1989, 1990, 1994, Santa Ynez Band of Chumash Indians in Collaboration with Richard B. Applegate 2007, Timbrook 2007, Walker and Johnson 1992, Weighill 2002). The interested reader should also look at *Native Americans on the Central Coast* (Black Gold Cooperative Library System in Collaboration with John Johnson 1997), which provides great historical photographs of the Chumash. The *Los Angeles Times*, the *Santa Barbara News Press*, and several local publications are also well-stocked with articles about the Chumash. The Santa Barbara Museum of Natural History, which has generated a great number of publications about the Chumash, has a website with an entire section dedicated to the tribe. The website for the Santa Ynez Band of Chumash Indians also holds a wealth of information that is readily available. There are two recent studies specifically about the Santa Ynez Chumash. Darian-Smith's book, *New Capitalists: Law, Politics, and Identity Surrounding Casino Gaming on Native Land* (2004), studies the cultural politics surrounding the construction of the new Chumash casino. Another valuable resource is the dissertation by the tribe's education director, Niki Sandoval. *Bridging Generations: American Indian Family Perceptions of Home/School Partnerships* (2007) studies the educational politics of the Santa Ynez Chumash in the home, in the tribe, and in local schools, examining how class, race, culture, and family involvement affect education.

p. 14   *The word "Chumash" comes from the word for shell bead money.* In addition to Malibu, several places names such as Mugu, Nipomo, Lompoc, and Pismo are Chumash in origin. There is some debate about the nature of Chumash society at the time of contact and during Spanish colonization, but it is generally agreed that there were about eight regional Chumash dialects between Malibu and San Luis Obispo (Richard Applegate as quoted in *LAT*, 6/16/03). Numbers for the pre-contact Chumash population vary, but estimates range from eighteen thousand to twenty-five thousand people living in approximately one hundred and fifty separate towns and villages, mostly along the coast; this population had developed over a period of some thirteen thousand years. Each of the approximately one hundred and fifty villages had its own political leader, a chief, who represented his group with natives and European invaders alike. Even during and through the end of the mission period in the 1830s, Indian communities within the mission system still had chiefs and a form of government. Much of this information is taken from an interview given by John Johnson, in Robinson (2004).

p. 15 *The large amount of historical and archeological literature about the Chumash.* There was village exogamy with patrilocal marriage—young women left their villages to marry, and there was a large amount of intermarriage as well as trade with non-Chumash groups. As Applegate states, "There was an annual round of festivals and rituals that drew people from adjacent areas, including from outside the Chumash speech area.... These fiestas were carefully staged in annual rotation and allowed people to attend a number of different events in widely separated areas. The fiestas created an opportunity for trade, intermarriage, reunions, social interaction, and the spread of news and ideas" (unpublished manuscript). Yet warfare apparently also played a role in Chumash society (see Gamble 2008).

p. 17 *But during the last few decades of Spanish colonialism...* Today, because of the different colonial powers in contact with the Chumash during the nineteenth century, Chumash cultural artifacts are found in museums in Russia, France, England, and elsewhere.

p. 17 *While some Indians joined the missions of their own will...* The quote "farmed out to local settlers and soldiers as a labor force for which the mission was paid in return" is taken from Darian-Smith (2004:73).

p. 17 *In contrast to the viceroyalties of Mexico and Peru...* Already falling from the approximately twenty-five thousand Chumash in pre-contact times to the 5,602 Chumash recorded at the five missions in 1805, the population fell even more rapidly in the nineteenth century. Because of disease, exploitation, and the suppression of an unsuccessful revolt in 1824, the Chumash were reduced to 1,182 by 1832. By the time of the first state census in 1852, the Chumash were less than six hundred (Walker and Johnson 1994:111). The decline of the Chumash population in the first half of the nineteenth century by almost 90 percent—and by 97 percent from the estimated pre-contact population—is similar in scope to the decimation of indigenous populations throughout the Americas following the arrival of Europeans in the sixteenth century. For the Chumash, as for the larger native population of the Americas centuries before, this population decline had the proportions of a holocaust.

p. 17 *Yet the population decline of those counted as "Chumash"*... As early as the late eighteenth century, the Chumash were already being forced to abandon their traditional religious practices and beliefs. An important part of the mission was to forcibly transculturate the Chumash into the Spanish way of life, while maintaining their servility. This continued after the secularization of the missions. Dana, who visited Santa Barbara in the 1830s, says, "The change in the condition of the Indians was, as may be supposed, only nominal: they are virtually slaves, as much as they ever were" (1986:233).

p. 18 *With Mexican independence came another wave of colonization.* The antireligious policies of the Mexican Republic undercut the mission system. The continuation of customary Chumash exogamous marriage practices (and no doubt now also the institution of concubinary relationships with powerful Spaniards and later Mexicans), led to considerable Chumash intermarriage with Spaniards and Mexicans. Chumash culture declined, although the Chumash themselves continued—some living together near the mission sites, others absorbed into the local ranching population (see, among others, Miller 1988). Post-mission life led in a couple of instances to Chumash cultural revitalization (see Johnson 1990:145).

p. 18 *The final stake in the heart of early Chumash culture came with the third wave of colonization...* Indigenous groups throughout North, Central, and South America are faced with cultural and political pressure to abandon their identities (Gelles 1998). Sometimes, it is the stigma attached to being "Indian" that accounts for the thousands of indigenous persons throughout countries such as Mexico, Guatemala, Peru, and Bolivia who have shed their indigenous languages, last names, dress, and general culture. In other cases, it is the risk of physical extermination. For example, during "La Matanza" in El Salvador, thousands of Indians were killed in a backlash to a revolt that occurred in the 1930s. Anyone with indigenous clothing or who spoke a native language was targeted. As a result, the indigenous people had to abandon their cultural identities or be killed. While not targeted for genocide like some groups in Northern California, there was a lot of pressure in the late nineteenth century for the Chumash to suppress their identity.

p. 18 *As with indigenous groups throughout the Americas subjected to cultural and political pressure.* The quote by Frances Snyder, "This isn't exactly a lost language," was taken from the *LAT*, 6/16/03.

p. 18 *At the time of the Spanish invasion, the Samala people (Ineseño Chumash) were made up...* See, among others, Gamble (2008) for more information.

p. 19   *But what stands out when looking at the valley against the flow of history...* Gamble's synthesis of the scholarship on Chumash society at the time of contact argues persuasively for the importance of the large mainland coastal settlements as a meeting place and an economic hub between the Channel Island populations, the "interior" (which includes the Santa Ynez Valley), and the coastal Chumash themselves (Gamble 2008:71-73).

p. 19   *During the Spanish colonial period, the valley remained on the periphery.* The quote "Chumash villages dotted the coastline, and the pueblo of Santa Barbara was no more than a ramshackle collection of huts clustered around the Presidio" is taken from Easton and Rye (1996:17).

p. 20   *And the Santa Ynez Valley was on the periphery of this periphery!* Refugio was the third pass. The San Marcos footpath was made into a mule trail in 1800 to allow improved access to the valley and its Indian populations (Johnson 1984:7).

p. 20   *Mission Santa Ynez was truly an outpost.* The quote "to effect the conversion of the remaining Chumash population in inland areas" is from Johnson (1989:369). Etling states that in 1836, the mission was prosperous, with 8,040 cattle, 1,923 sheep, 343 horses, 987 fruit trees, and forty-five mules. At the mission, along with the church and as part of its courtyard, was a blacksmith shop for the vaqueros (cow-boys) and other uses, a potter's shop, facilities for weaving, a storehouse, guardhouse, and quarters for the soldiers and their families as well as for the priests and members of the religious order (see the Mission Santa Ynez website, and Etling 2005:280).

p. 20   *In the first half of the nineteenth century, Mission Santa Ynez was the valley* The nearest rancho until then was Rancho Refugio, a huge coastal estate and the first rancho granted in Santa Barbara. When it was raided by pirates in 1818, the owner fled over the coastal mountains to Mission Santa Ynez (Easton and Rye 1996:23), his family house of worship. In the 1840s, the population was so low and the cattle herds so vast that travelers were allowed "to kill a steer for food, so long as they left the hide behind for the owner" (Ibid: 26). Here it bears noting that much of the ranch culture and land use traditions that developed in the Santa Ynez Valley came from traditions that the Moors of northern Africa had brought to rural Spain over several centuries and that were later brought over to the Americas. As Isaacson puts it, "In these unpopulated areas of the Iberian Peninsula, livestock operations utilized horse-men, hot-iron branding, and large scale herding techniques in the management of cattle. The cattle were not tame, but, in fact, semi-wild... Other more subtle strands of the Spanish tradition also became deeply woven in California's ranching culture" (Isaacson and Moore 2004:1). This culture continues on today in the valley, especially in those large ranches where "cattle roam freely over large expanses of semi-arid grazing land" (Ibid:1).

p. 20   *As we saw above, the Chumash population in general, from 1805 to 1852, declined almost...* These population numbers are taken from Walker and Johnson (1994:111). "A small cemetery next to the [Santa Ynez] mission cathedral holds the remains of about 1,700 Indians, marked by crumbled tombstones and splintered crosses covered in moss" (*LAT*, 12/3/04). According to Norris (2008), between 1804 and 1850 there were only 1,631 baptisms, 497 marriages, and 1,632 deaths for the American Indian inhabitants of the valley at the mission. The "white" totals—and here we are talking about non-Indians, presumably most of them of Spanish descent—were only forty-seven baptisms, eight marriages, and fifteen deaths.

p. 21   *One instance is the Chumash revolt of 1824, which began at Mission Santa Ynez.* Two Chumash Indians, one from Santa Ynez and one from Santa Barbara, stated the reason for the conflict—a rumor that the Spaniards were going to massacre Indians—to anthropologist J.P. Harrington almost a century later (Hudson 1980). The Hispanic version is that it began as a result of the tensions arising from the fight for Mexican independence around 1810, when the missions were forced to become self-sustaining. From 1821 to 1824, the soldiers were not paid, and the Chumash were forced to supply the soldiers and their families. This was part of the growing mistreatment of the Chumash from the turn of the century, and supplying the soldiers became an onerous and increasingly coercive burden. According to this version (see Mission Santa Ynez website as well as other sources such as Miller 1988:32), a Chumash man visiting from La Purísima was seized and flogged, and this act set off the revolt.

p. 21   *The physical coercion and brutality that underlay the colonial system (see Miller 1988:33).* A decade later, in 1834, a Yankee expedition coming down the valley from Monterey "found 700 Chumash who spoke Spanish and farmed the land.... They had been joined by other fugitives and prospered on their own with a cultural mixture of Spanish and traditional ways" (Miller 1988:39).

p. 22   *The first land grant in the Santa Ynez Valley was given in 1836.* The quote "resembled simple homesteads more than the rich estates of popular imagination" is taken from Easton and Rye (1996:30).

p. 22 *Although a couple of Chumash men received short-lived ranchos.* Two Iñeseno Chumash received large ranchos: Antonino Silimunajait, originally from Santa Barbara but married at Mission Santa Ynez, where he was a resident, received Rancho Saca in 1838. He and his wife were later killed at their rancho by raiding Indians that came from the southern San Joaquin Valley (Johnson 1990:162). Marcelino Cuinait, the chief of the Santa Ynez Chumash, received Rancho Alamo Pintado in 1843, but it was purchased by a powerful non-Indian a few years later (Johnson 1990) and it did not bring him prosperity (Easton and Rye 1996:28). Sixteen smaller tracts of land were granted to other Chumash heads of household in Santa Ynez for the purposes of cultivation in 1843; the Indians were not allowed to sell or lease them, but they could pass them on to their heirs. These ranchos were small homesteads, not even villages, with tiny populations. One early exception was Rancho San Carlos de Jonata, which was developed by Rufus Thompson Buell, who bought and developed the ranch after the great drought of 1863–64. The ranch had "a blacksmith shop, a cheese factory, a general store, a schoolhouse, and a post office" (Ibid:39). These lands eventually became what today are Solvang and Buellton.

p. 22 *In sum, four key points can be made...* The quote "fared no better in their freedom than they had under the bondage of the mission system" is taken from Miller (1988:37). While the so-called pure-blood Chumash continued to decrease through intermarriage with Spaniards and Mexicans, "those Chumash who were forced to adapt at the cost of their culture survived" (Miller 1988:38). Some Chumash, however, continued to be groomed as culture-bearers.

p. 22 *The valley continued to be on the periphery...* This was largely because of the rugged Santa Ynez Mountains, which were "the only barrier in the road systems already existing between San Francisco and Los Angeles" (quote is from Tompkins 1982:21). The only entries to the valley from the south were the footpaths of Chumash origin. "El Camino Real, the storied 'King's Highway' of Spanish times, was in reality a mere foot trail" (Ibid:21). Prior to 1868, the valley was largely outside the stage network and "did not have a road that even the sturdiest mud wagon could traverse" (Ibid:28).

p. 23 *In 1855, the final Santa Ynez Chumash families who had remained were forced off of the mission and their allotted lands.* See Johnson (1990).

p. 23 *But the situation of the ranchos changed dramatically.* For more detail, see Norris (2008:15) and Easton and Rye (1996:44).

p. 23   *As one source nicely puts it...* Quote taken from Easton and Rye (1996:44).

p. 24   *This is backed by the testimony of the elderly daughter...* While Jane Hollister Wheelright herself worked against prejudice in her later life, she makes clear the influences that were passed down to her through her family, and the extreme prejudice that Indians were subjected to in this region. Quotes are from Wheelright (1988:23-25).

p. 24   *In 1859, a network of stagecoach roads in the Santa Ynez Valley began....* The quote ("augment the private thoroughfares...") is from Tompkins, 1982, who states, "The cuts and fills were created by the use of the sweat, muscle, and black powder of the Chinese coolie gangs whose bivouac near the Santa Ynez River is still called Chinese camp" (Tompkins 1982:32).

p. 24   *For the next several decades, until 1901...* See Norris 2008:29, Tompkins 1982. From Santa Barbara to Matteis, it was an eight-hour trip on the six-horse teams if there was no inclement weather or robbery. Even after the train connected San Francisco to Los Angeles in 1901, horses and horse-driven vehicles remained integral to life in the valley for transportation, farming, and moving supplies and produce.

p. 24   *Yet the train's arrival from the north and its final stop in Los Olivos...* For nice photographs of this time, see Norris (2008). As with the stage roads, Chinese workers completed the railroad; the Chinese also graded the streets for Los Olivos. Many stayed on as local ranch cooks, and both Los Olivos and Santa Ynez had Chinese laundries (Norris 2008, Etling 2005).

p. 24   *The valley towns began to grow quickly...* "All railroad companies, while working their way across America, followed a similar pattern: acquire right of way by purchase or government incentive, start a 'local' newspaper for publicity concerning the soon-to-arrive 'paradise,' build a hotel, offer very attractive fares, plat a town site, widely advertise a picnic or barbecue, and—hopefully—auction lots" (Norris 2008:37). The information that twenty-nine buildings were constructed in the first year alone is taken from Norris (2008:91). "Santa Ynez did boom for a time in the 1880s with a number of businesses in operation, ranging from saloons and blacksmith shops to general mercantile stores, a pharmacy, a feed store, millinery and barber shops, and real estate agents" (Introduction, Santa Ynez Historical Calendar 2006). So, too, in 1888, Los Olivos had a post office, two general merchandising stores, a drug store, a machine shop, several saloons, and a livery stable.

p. 25   *But local hopes for a train route through Santa Ynez were dashed.* This information comes largely from Tompkins (1982:38).

p. 25   *The foregoing shows that when the Chumash Reservation was established at the turn of the twentieth century...* The Montanaro ranch in Los Olivos included a small store on the property and another in Santa Ynez; the ranch account book from 1894–1895 "lists 159 customers" (Norris 2008:15).

p. 25   *At this time, Los Olivos and Santa Ynez were just tiny communities...* The information on the Buell ranch is taken from Cragg (2006). The ranch was a self-sufficient operation with "a post office, a public store, and a blacksmith" (Etling 2005: 284; see also Norris 2008:91), but was still a tiny settlement. The quote about Las Cruces is taken from Cragg (2008:109), and the quote about the port at Gaviota is taken from Cragg (2008:97).

p. 26   *The influx of Danish settlers in 1911 added another flavor.* Some of this information comes from the Santa Ynez Historical Calendar (2006). The colony was dedicated to the preservation of Danish arts, customs, and culture through a folk school, the Danish Lutheran church, and the maintenance of spoken Danish. Some of the newly arrived Danes shipped catalog homes to the Gaviota wharf and then hauled them to Solvang (Cragg 2008:14), while others built them out of lumber that came by rail to Los Olivos. Many of the Danish settlers lived in Los Olivos while they built their houses. The assertion that early photos reveal nothing Danish about the town's architecture comes from Cragg (2008:7). We are talking about a small population at this time. A photograph from the early years of the Danish settlement shows the mission separated by some fields from the town of Solvang, and a religious procession with perhaps a hundred people. It is captioned, "Practicing Catholics and the Lutheran Danes join together for the annual Easter sojourn from the Easter Cross to Mission Santa Ynez. Although the Danes founded Solvang to establish a Danish Lutheran church, they had no objection to maintaining an ecumenical relationship with their Catholic neighbors" (Ibid:16). It is safe to say that many of those Catholic neighbors were, at least in part, of Chumash descent.

p. 26   *Yet the Danes kept a distinct identity.* See (Norris 2008:91). The quote "Some of the locals from the surrounding towns probably attended these early events, but for the most part they were hard to follow because all of the singing and speaking was in Danish" is from Cragg (2008:75).

p. 26 *The automobile had a major impact...* After 1915, cars replaced horses for mail transport and for busing school children (Norris 2008: 29). In 1920, Buellton was officially named (Santa Ynez Historical Calendar, 2006), and, in 1924, Andersen's Electrical Café, the precursor to the famous Pea Soup Andersen's Restaurant, was established there. Buellton, between 1920 and the 1940s, was better known as a destination than Solvang (Cragg 2008:116). For information about Las Cruces, see Tompkins (1982:21).

p. 27 *The valley remained rather sedate until World War II.* The information for this paragraph comes from the Santa Ynez Historical Calendar (2006). Also in 1930, the high school in Santa Ynez graduated twenty students (today the high school graduates over two hundred and fifty annually). A report by the California State Department of Education written in 1931 states that there were 294 elementary students in the different schools of the valley. In 1932, Midland School, a ranch school with "needs, not wants" as its organizing principle, was founded outside the town of Los Olivos, and its faculty and their children later helped found other schools in the valley (such as the Family School and Dunn School).

p. 28 *After World War II, especially with the publication of an article about Solvang in the Saturday Evening Post...* The quote that the Danes "capitalized on the attention by developing an annual celebration called Danish Days" is from Cragg (2008:8). The quote "car crazy Californians took to the open road and discovered the Santa Ynez Valley" is from Cragg (2008:43). It was soon evident that the Danes could commodify and capitalize on their ethnicity. Solvang "was certainly more Danish in language and culture prior to World War II, but after the war, Danish architecture permeated the town, including windmills," which are "Americanized interpretations designed primarily to decorate the town" (Ibid:62-63). Today, there is still a sizable population of people of Danish descent, and many local businesses are still run by them.

Two   From Powerless to Powerful: The Chumash in the Twentieth Century and Today

The epigram is from the *SYVN* (12/12/06).

p. 42 *The Santa Ynez Band formerly tied to the mission was officially recognized...* (Santa Ynez Band of Chumash Indians Website). It is one of the smallest Indian reservations in California, with only 127 acres; it is located adjacent to the Zanja de Cota Creek, which used to carry water to the gristmill of Mission Santa Ynez (and which also used to be the dividing line between the Diocese of Monterey and the Diocese of Los Angeles and San Diego [*SBNP* 1967 10/4/67]). The information about a 1930 census is from the Santa Ynez Historical Calendar, 2006. Other Chumash groups such as the Coastal Chumash have sought official recognition for some time but have yet to achieve it.

p. 44   *The tribe's relative lack of power again comes through loud and clear.* The Mrs. James Pace quote is from the *SBNP* (10/4/67).

p. 48   *Esther and several other Chumash were some of the hundreds of American Indian children...* Sandoval's quote that the native students "spent most of the day engaged in vocational curriculum that focused on domestic work" (that is, skills associated with laundress, waitress, and housekeeper), is from Sandoval (2007:20). Although Esther does not have altogether unpleasant memories of the place, many other Chumash do. Dominica Valencia tells me how hard it was for her father and his brother and two sisters. Her uncle had an especially bad time, running away repeatedly from the school. The people Sandoval interviewed all spoke of the loneliness they experienced and how the administrators fostered mistrust between Chumash and Navajo students. "They made us cut their hair. We were scared. We were afraid to go to sleep. We thought they might come and get us" (Ibid:12). It is clear that, as at other "Indian schools" (see Cooper 1999, Trafzer et al. 2006), the conditions could be rough and there was no respect for native culture. The official website of the Sherman Institute, founded in the nineteenth century in Riverside, California, by the United States government, says that its purpose was "to assimilate Native Americans into the mainstream society." Hundreds of American-Indian children were removed from their homes and communities to be taught a trade and to be educated in a way that would have them conform to Euro-American society. "Because of Bureau [of Indian Affairs] policies, students did not return home for several years; many of them died and were buried in the school cemetery.... They just happened to live in a time when people in positions of power believed the best solution to a changing American culture was to gather these children together into a military boarding school, to change them, Americanize them, and train them to become citizens within the culture in power. It seems that our country's leaders chose to ignore one thing: these children already had a culture."

p. 49   *Language is one window into culture loss and retrieval...* Applegate says, "For example, the word for paternal grandmother is *naanaa* and apparently it is still a custom in a lot of native families to call granny *naanaa*, but little things like that. At the very best it might be like third generation Jews who know a few words of Yiddish that they use in their conversation. And also because there is so much literature on the Chumash that people have read, there was a secondary effect of retaining the language, because a lot of people know the word *haku*, 'hello,' or *tomol* for boat. But not because they learned it from their folks but because everybody has read *The Eye of the Flute* and *Decembers Child*." As far as language, the last fluent native speaker of Ineseño Chumash died a long time ago. Some Chumash remember their grandparents speaking at least some phrases of Chumash in mid-century. One tribal member states that her grandma sang songs in Chumash, "and my aunt and Mom still remember the tunes." This person says that when her grandmother spoke Chumash, she thought, "What's wrong with her? It sounded like gibberish to me."

p. 52   *Nevertheless, conditions began to change for the better in the late 1960s...* "The Santa Ynez Indian Reservation, lacking adequate water, sanitation, electricity, and decent housing, seeks to pull itself up by the bootstraps.... For 25 years the Indians have appealed to the Bureau of Indian Affairs of the U.S. Department of the Interior to do something to alleviate the potentially dangerous situation. Their requests have been bypassed, postponed indefinitely or ignored completely, according to spokesmen for the Santa Ynez Indian band" (*SBNP* 10/4/67; 10/10/67).

p. 52   *As a result, economic conditions for the Chumash started to improve...* Kathy Marshall described the old clinic to me. "It was a home, a trailer home; it was not even fixed up to look like an office. There was a kitchen, a living room, bed room, the doctor's office was the master bedroom, there was a kitchen counter—it was a house! They didn't do any construction work to make it look like a clinic because there was no funding for it." While they did get grants from Indian Health Services, the care was minimal and Chumash would have to go to the Indian Health Clinic in Santa Barbara for dental work or anything serious.

p. 53   *The appearance of the bingo parlor in the mid-1980s began to generate some employment and benefits...* By December 2001, when the tribe held three days of festivities to celebrate one hundred years as a federally recognized tribe (*SMT*, 12/10/01), they could afford nationally recognized musicians and comedians. A tented structure served as the casino until the new casino and resort was built in 2003 with the tribe investing $157 million (*LAT*, 12/03/05).

p. 54   *The Santa Ynez Band of Chumash Indians is one of several groups of Chumash...* Although, in the past, the casino revenues resulting from federal recognition at times generated tension among Chumash groups, they have also allowed "the recognized Chumash tribe to revitalize and promote its cultural heritage, and this self confidence has seeped into the consciousness of other Chumash peoples" (Darian-Smith 2004:76). As seen in chapter six, there is currently cooperation between the Santa Ynez Band and other Chumash groups in revitalizing culture and in symbolically and ritually reclaiming Chumash history and cultural patrimony.

p. 54   *Today, while many Chumash live off-reservation, "approximately three hundred people reside on the reservation, which is located on 126 acres."* This quote is from Sandoval (2007:8). The information about members and descendants is from the *LAT* (12/03/05). Members enjoy monthly per capita payouts. But many more individuals benefit directly from the casino revenues. While Sandoval reports that "more than 600 lineal descendants who are 1/8 blood quantum or less are also recognized by the tribal government" (2007:6), other descendants with a lesser blood quantum also qualify for educational and other benefits.

p. 55   *The mixture with the Spanish-speaking world is complex...* In short, this linguistic pattern has been around for a long time, and connects the Chumash to indigenous people throughout Spanish America—that is, countries formerly controlled by the Spanish Empire. At the same time, the Chumash have intermarried with other groups such as the Filipinos, who settled in northern Santa Barbara County. But the Chumash have an especially strong relationship to Latino identities because of intermarriage and long-standing ties with Mexicans in the area and south of the border. I am indebted to conversations with Richard Applegate about the ways Chumash English and Spanish differ from the English and Spanish spoken by other residents in the valley.

p. 57   *Some of the opposition voices are reasonable.* When Highway 154 was named the Chumash Highway (see Robinson 2008a), these critics decried it as an attempt to advertise the casino rather than to reclaim Chumash heritage. We will return to these debates in chapter eight; in the intermediate chapters we will explore at length the incredible strides that the tribe has made in educating its members and descendants and in reclaiming, revitalizing, and safeguarding its culture and cultural patrimony.

p. 58   *The tribe has also established the Santa Ynez Band of Chumash Indians Foundation.* Cited from a commentary by Richard Gomez, the vice chairman of the tribe, in *SYVN* 5/ 24/2012, "Help Cook up Help for Seniors." In addition, the tribe has contributed over $3 million to the local high school to refurbish its football field and stadium and over a million dollars to a local hospital. It also helps many non-profits in the area, as discussed later in the book. As Gomez puts it, "In good times and in bad, the Santa Ynez Chumash Indian Foundation has stepped up to help our neighbors throughout the county." The goal is to make the community "a better place for all of its residents, placing particular value on activities and programs that expand opportunities for the least advantaged, protect our environment or enhance the lives of youth."

Three   Current Cultural Politics in the Valley

Epigram taken from Eve Darian-Smith (2004:5).

p. 63   *Nevertheless, that the tribe has had an antagonistic relationship...* In this chapter, we look at the domination of the Chumash on a more subtle cultural level. The key question that needs to be asked when looking at the politics of culture is: which cultures get represented, valued, validated, and publicly celebrated—and which do not? When we look at the ritual calendar, the symbols that are mobilized in different local celebrations, and the resulting ways in which history is made in the valley, we can see that white heritage is dominant and that other groups, including the Chumash, are largely excluded. One way into the differences found in the "imagined community" (see Anderson 1983, Smith 1982) of the Santa Ynez Valley is to look at local civic celebrations and the festival calendar, as well as at local rituals, museums, schools, textbooks, and newspapers.

p. 63   *The valley has been multicultural for a long time.* There are great regional differences among those of Mexican descent living in the valley. Although many families hail from the Mexican states of Jalisco, Michoacan, and Guerrero, others come from Oaxaca.

p. 64   *They say that history is written by the victors...* For example, across Highway 246 from the reservation, in the small town of Santa Ynez itself, established in 1882, the annual celebration known as Santa Ynez Day commemorates the founding of the town with a number of cultural activities, such as live music, vendor booths, a parade, and a "tortilla toss" (not a Mexican tradition). Although the Chumash had the first settlement in what today is Santa Ynez—being relocated there more than thirty years before the town was founded—there is little to no acknowledgement of the Chumash during Santa Ynez Day.

p. 65   *Exclusion, whether through ritual celebration or outright racism and overt prejudice...* Sometimes it's based on class, as when wealthy residents exchange insults with striking supermarket workers. Sometimes it's based on race, as when a local storeowner cheers against the Lakers because the opposing team has more white players. Sometimes it's based on class and race together, as when one of the valley's elementary schools keeps a local nonprofit from helping its Latino immigrant students.

p. 66   *Things have gotten much better over the years.* But I do not want to downplay the antagonism that is experienced today by some Chumash and Latinos, sometimes in the form of overt racism. Almost all the Chumash and Latinos I know have an anecdote (or several) about discrimination at school or in social settings. And as a white person, I have heard negative comments about Latinos, some made out of ignorance and some downright racist.

p. 66   *When I asked her whether the situation has improved for the Chumash kids...* Sometimes the prejudice is even more overt. While shopping at a local market, Frances was yelled at by one of the Chumash opponents. He then asked her with a smirk, "How does it feel, Frances, to be the only brown person living in your neighborhood?" She felt threatened and called the sheriff's office; she then hired security to patrol her house while her husband was out of town. Eventually she moved back to her house in Northern California. Another Chumash woman, Dominica Valencia, tells me, "You know, prejudice is something you've been taught since you were a child. You don't just suddenly say, 'I'm prejudiced' against a certain person.' I think that's what it is. And jealousy. There are so many things they tell us that we're not capable of doing. It's just a few. The majority of the people don't say that; it's just a handful and they're enough to rock the boat."

p. 66   *Stereotypes of the Chumash, and current debates about the tribe and its casino...* Some of the stereotypes regarding the Chumash have been admirably brought to light by Darian-Smith (2004), who studied the different issues and debates surrounding the Chumash establishment of their new casino in the early 2000s. Darian-Smith finds that "local resistance [to the Chumash] is often couched in implicit and explicit racist terms particular to Native Americans." The quote "The implicit message is: If 'they' were equal to 'us,' so many of them wouldn't still be living in squalid poverty" is taken from Darian-Smith (2004:17).

p. 67 *The other stereotype, that of the "noble savage," is even more insidious.* The quote "if Native Americans really loved the land and had a spiritual affinity with nature, as they supposedly do, then how could they possibly be advocating for a large building development on their own reservation? This argument harks back to a romanticized stereotype of Native Americans as being, in effect, remnants of a prehistoric age—spiritual, communal, untouched and unblemished by the corruption of modern society" is from Darian-Smith (2004:92). And the quote from a public official, "They have, you know, taken up a really beautiful legacy of basketry and tommel (sic) building, and really interesting lifestyles and sort of erased it with one fell swoop," is also taken from Darian-Smith (2004:92). For a humorous yet poignant view of the role of stereotypes in American Indian identity formation, see Alexie 2007.

p. 67 *This stereotype reveals an amazing ignorance of the Chumash's previous poverty...* The quote from Eve Darian-Smith is found in her book (2004:5).

p. 67 *A prime example of this mentality is found in a 2004 paid advertisement* (SBNP, 6/11/04). Written by musician and pop star Sir Elton John's songwriting partner, Bernie Taupin, and signed by other local celebrities such as David Crosby, Bo Derek, and Doc Severinsen, Taupin concludes that the Chumash are bringing about the end of a pastoral wonderland and must be defeated: "If we lose I can already feel the tears of the hawks as they circle what was once a green and promised land."

p. 68 *So, these are the choices, according to these two views...* The quote "The underlying assumption of these attitudes is that Indian peoples are only truly Indian if they are poor, out of sight and out of mind on faraway reservations, and are not part of mainstream society" is from Darian-Smith (2004:5).

p. 68 *While their voice is not as loud and shrill.* See also Darian-Smith 2004. Many organizations, such as the NAACP of Santa Barbara County, also support the Chumash and their endeavors. The president of the NAACP likes how the casino benefits Indians directly, and because gambling is viewed as a business apart from cultural practices, she sees no negative impact on their culture. Another person who supports the Chumash talks to the institutionalized racism in the valley: "I have heard with shame the bigotry about what is going on here.... The tribe was given one of the scrappiest pieces of property here in this valley, and everybody knows it.... It's not just the past generations, it's the current generation. How could all of us forget so quickly what this reservation looked like just a few years ago? The county roads on the reservation were a disgrace. There was no money to upgrade the homes because many tribal members eked out a living bordering on the poverty level. Where were all the so-called 'concerned citizens' then? For that matter, I don't recall seeing any of you concerned citizens when the tribe celebrated its 100th anniversary just a few months ago. You were invited" (in Darian-Smith 2004:84). We return to these politics in chapter eight.

Four   Education and Marginalization

The epigram is from Sandoval (2007:19).

p. 73   *The first part of this book used broad strokes to sketch the historical experience...* Frankly, it is hard to keep abreast of all the ever-expanding education and culture programs of the Santa Ynez Chumash. This list of Chumash accomplishments is necessarily partial and, by the time this book is published, many new initiatives will be in place.

p. 73   *This second part of the book relies a great deal on Chumash narratives.* Hearing the voices of those who have no voice, those often left out of the history books, allows us to rewrite the history written by the "victors," that is, by the dominant society. At the same time, it is important to point out that there is variation in the "Chumash experience," that is, different Chumash individuals experience local society and schools differently. And while I interviewed several Chumash individuals involved in education and culture, mine is only a partial sample and there are many more voices to be heard, stories to be told. Yet the voices recorded here speak for a wider group of Chumash who have experienced similar processes. Indeed, when it comes to education, these testimonies reflect larger trends in American Indian communities throughout California and the nation. In her review of the literature, Sandoval notes that nationwide just 18 percent of American Indians ages eighteen through twenty-four were enrolled in secondary education, compared to 42 percent for whites, in 2005. American Indians were awarded .8 percent of the college degrees awarded that year, compared to 67 percent for whites. While over 620,000 people self-identified as American Indian in the state of California in 2000, only 302 American Indian students were conferred degrees by the University of California in the years 2003–2004 (Sandoval 2007:2). Part of this has to do with the absence of California Indians in the curricula. Sandoval notes, "The only statewide curriculum standard that includes American Indians is in the fourth grade when public schools learn about early California history. As California Indians are central to the story of colonization and the establishment of the mission system, students statewide are exposed briefly to the circumstances faced by indigenous peoples during this period. The inclusion of Native peoples in the California curriculum standards stops in the mission period. This is a disservice to all students" (2007:19).

p. 74   *Longstanding elements of segregation, prejudice, and open discrimination...* Now in her seventies, and sporting a bear claw tattoo and a red bandana, Adelina is the spiritual leader of the tribe. She is also a cultural revivalist, a compassionate defender of indigenous rights, and a traditionalist who has carried out rituals and ceremonies throughout Chumash territory and as far away as Panama and South Africa. She is also consulted for her knowledge by local museums, the Forestry Service, and the State Park system. One of twenty-six elders statewide to be awarded the UC Berkeley Senior Leadership for California Award, Adelina is also the previous chair of the Elders Committee. Her fluency in Spanish, her knowledge of the territory and sacred landscape of the Chumash, her literacy in Chumash history and culture, and her many diverse experiences make her an excellent ambassador for the Chumash people, both with other tribes and with institutions of the dominant society. Forced to marry at fifteen, Adelina had seven children by the time she was twenty-one. In addition to her other responsibilities, Adelina is a veritable matriarch with, at last count, thirty-six grandchildren and thirty-two great-grandchildren.

p. 74   *Chumash kids living on the reservation, as Niki Sandoval found in her study of educational politic...* See especially Sandoval (2007:13, 14, 59). The testimonies of individuals from the reservation that I gathered corroborate her findings.

p. 76   *Yet the discrimination experienced by many students...* The quote "to serve students with behavioral, learning, and physical differences who were not well served in mainstream classrooms" is from Sandoval (2007:12).

p. 79   *Exclusion and discrimination was tied to an absence of Chumash history.* The ways in which the history taught in public education excludes the Chumash and other ethnic groups dovetails with the way that ethnic diversity is celebrated in the ritual calendar of the valley.

p. 81   *Niki Sandoval, who has both personal experience and a professional interest in the topic...* Sandoval earned a BA from Pepperdine University, a master's from George

Washington University, and her PhD from the University of California at Santa Barbara (see Sandoval 2007).

p. 82   *Her sister Carmen, now one of the Chumash language apprentices, fared even worse…*
A disproportionate number of native students such as Carmen were placed in special education (Sandoval 2007:62). While it has gotten better, in 2006 a local elementary school in the valley was still placing 24 percent of its native students in special education (Sandoval 2007:62).

p. 83   *This pattern was experienced by Chumash at other schools in the larger Central Coast region.* That Frances went on to higher education was almost by chance. "At first I didn't know that there *were* opportunities. I remember sitting in Mr. Mussard's psychology class in high school watching my black friend, Lynda Stone, filling out college applications. She asked me what colleges I was applying to. I told her that I wasn't going to college because my family couldn't afford it. She looked shocked and said, 'What do you think financial aid is for?' She also told me that I could qualify for scholarships. I was surprised and said, 'I could?' She said, 'You run circles around these white kids here. You're much smarter than they are. Of course you could win scholarships. Hell, you could win them all!' It was that conversation that got me thinking about the possibility of college. Before that, the idea of college didn't even enter my mind because it seemed like it was so out of the realm of reality for me. Getting a job—that was the goal for everyone. Getting a job, getting married, having children—that was viewed as success back then, not going to college." But Frances went on and received a BA degree from San Francisco State University in journalism and her master's degree from Stanford in communication. Going deeper into Frances's narrative is instructive for comprehending the forces arrayed against most Chumash. "My father was a farm laborer who made less than ten thousand dollars a year and my mother made less than that as a nurse's aide in a convalescent hospital. To them, college represented an enormous expense that they couldn't possibly afford." Even though Frances received scholarships, financial aid, and a grant from the Bureau of Indian Affairs, she also had to work full-time through both her undergraduate and graduate degrees. Frances tells me, "There's practically an entire decade of music that I missed because I spent all my time either in school or at work. Today when performers from the eighties come to our resort, I often don't know their music. Heart, Pat Benatar, Steve Miller, the Go-Go's—I don't remember their music. People always laugh at me because it was like I was MIA for an entire decade."

p. 83   *Tonie Flores contrasts her own experience in the high school...* Tonie says, "I think it's easier to be Chumash now, because the Mexican race has a better relationship with the high school. They're more honored because there are more Mexicans in high school now." Although a Chicano studies program has been established, no American Indian clubs or studies are offered by the high school.

p. 84   *While Chumash educational initiatives and the newfound economic and political power...* Antagonism toward Chumash kids, largely because of the casino and their newfound wealth, sometimes takes place even in grade school. Leslie states, "I just heard last week that the elementary school is like that, too. I heard it out of the mouth of an eight-year-old girl. I was just like, 'Oh, my gosh. I thought, *Okay, yeah, it's hard in high school;, even the security officers are harassing our Indian kids*. But to hear it out of the mouth of an eight-year-old that it's happening in the K-8, that really concerned me, because I thought that would be a safe haven for them up until high school. And then, you know, we can really bolster them."

Five   Knowledge is Power: New Educational Opportunities

Epigram is from an interview the author conducted with Nakia Zavalla.

p. 88   *The Chumash Education Department is made up of the education programs direc-tor and the Education Committee.* The Education Committee is one of several stand-ing committees. It is made up of "seven elected members of the tribe whose vision includes strengthening the connection within the family, the tribe and the commu-nity, expanding individual horizons and driving student success" (Santa Ynez Band of Chumash Indians Website). The committee members keep a close watch on how different programs are running and often contribute directly to them. Others com-mittees include the Business Committee, Ballot Committee, Elders Committee, Enrollment Committee, Health Board, Housing Commission, and the Pow Wow Committee. The Education Committee has "a mailing list of more than 500 individ-uals or families who are tribal community members" (Sandoval 2007:7). According to one Education Committee member, the education programs have already helped over a thousand members and descendants.

p. 90   *Besides the tutoring funds and resources, the tribe provides significant funding...* The tribe has offered partial tuition reimbursement for independent schools since 1998 (Sandoval 2007:9), and this has had a positive impact on Chumash education overall.

p. 90   *Just as the tribe has provided a strong and well-funded support system for its youth...*
Ironically, some critics of the Chumash fault them for being relatively uneducated compared with others in the valley. But this view ignores history and the cultural pressures
militating against the Chumash for generations. The ability to attend college says something about your socioeconomic class, family income, and capacity to read and write
English. The quote "Native Americans have more difficulty attending college than most
and for reasons that have nothing to do with the quality or capacity of individuals" is from
Darian-Smith (2004:17). She continues, "Rather, they have been subjected to long-standing
discriminatory laws, forced to live on faraway reservations with little money for transportation, clothes, and books, and have had to take local, often poor-paying jobs close to home
at an earlier age in order to supplement low family incomes" (Darian-Smith 2004:17).

p. 94   *To reach the goal of increased parental and school support...* The program was con-
ceived of as being not just for American-Indian students but more broadly for low-
income, first-generation college students. Although many of the Chumash families in
Santa Ynez no longer qualify as "low-income," they are still a marginalized community
in need of service. In 2007, Leslie Koda had eleven mentors, and in 2008, seventeen
mentors. Santa Ynez Valley Union High School had fifty American Indian students in
2007, including some non-Chumash, according to Leslie. Of those cases, the program
took on eleven students, many of whom were struggling with their core courses, especially English. Koda has also organized workshops for the students, such as one in which
an American-Indian author came and gave a reading of her work, which was followed by
a writing workshop.

p. 98   *In addition to her duties as a language apprentice, Kathy has been working hard at the
state level.* One of eleven members of this committee, she and her colleagues reviewed
the curriculum for different grade levels and also acted as an advisory committee for
American-Indian grants coming through the state. She says that she has learned a
great deal from her fellow committee members, many of whom have decades of experience with American-Indian education.

Six   Cultural and Linguistic Revitalization
Epigram is from an interview the author conducted with Virginia Garcia.

p. 106   *Yet there were increasingly strong political and cultural pressures...* According to
Applegate, the Chumash speech community began to suffer as soon as the missions

were founded because of population loss, the disruption of community through relocation, mixed marriages, and the stigmatization of Indian identity and language. "It could be dangerous to be perceived as Indian. The Chumash spoke Spanish and bore Spanish names and many passed as Hispanic during this time" (Applegate 2007:9). And, as we saw in chapter four, in the first half of the twentieth century, "the United States government made a concerted effort to suppress native culture, including forcibly removing Indian children to boarding schools where they would learn English—and be punished for using their native languages" (Ibid). There was thus little motivation for passing the language on to succeeding generations. And yet, as the tribe's introduction to the new Samala/English dictionary states, "Many tribal members remember hearing Samala words throughout their childhood. In spite of the many attempts to abolish the Samala Chumash language, it remained quietly in the background throughout the years as a word here and a phrase there passed from generation to generation" (2007:5).

p. 106   *Today, the Elders Committee and the Cultural Programs Department...* For example, the language program originally began with the Education Department, as did the summer program, Camp Kalawashaq. But there has been considerable overlap in these programs, with the elders and Cultural Programs Department fully involved.

p. 107   *The revival of Samala is nothing less than remarkable...* Some of this information comes from interviews and personal communication with Richard Applegate. The quote that Maria's grandmother "had been *esclava de la mission*" is from Laird (1975:18). The quote "The vessel of the old culture was broken" is from Laird (1975:112), and the quote that Maria treated Harrington "with the indulgence that one would accord a child or a harmless madman" is from Laird (1975:17). Nevertheless, "It is believed that no other anthropologist gathered such a staggering quantity of material in the field as did Harrington" (Lawton, in Laird 1975:viii). He shipped literally tons of field notes to the Bureau of American Ethnology and this work has helped not just the Chumash but other tribes as well.

p. 109   *The apprentice program began with five of Applegate's most dedicated students.* Applegate tells me that the apprentice program began because, in addition to having standard language classes, "it was important for members of the community to have a grasp of the language which they own themselves and can share with other members of the community. They're well known members of the community, too, and they're approachable in a way I am not." The apprentices are not volunteers; they are funded through the Elders Committee and are paid to go out and teach in the community. Applegate explains, "They are producing teaching materials that I review and they are doing classes. There's culture night. They're working a lot with the kids in the summer program." The language apprentices work with Chumash kids of all ages, meet regularly with the elders, and give presentations to schools in the region. They have reached hundreds of children and are spreading the use of the language through different social forums.

p. 110 *In addition to providing information on vocabulary and grammatical structure...* The quote "well over a hundred narratives in the Samala language..." comes from Applegate (2007:11). Much of the additional information in this paragraph was provided by Richard Applegate in interviews and personal communication. Because these texts contain information of a sensitive or sacred nature, it is the tribe that controls and monitors the dissemination of these texts. So far, the newly translated texts have gone only to the elders and language apprentices. Applegate tells me that the texts are "impenetrable to someone who does not know the language. What I am doing is bringing it back and making it available to the people." He hopes that someday the apprentices themselves will be able to transcribe and translate Harrington's difficult manuscripts.

p. 112 *A powerful new tool for the language program and for cultural revitalization...* The Education Committee decided that a dictionary not only would support the language program but would preserve a part of Chumash traditions and culture forever. Applegate generated his first grammar and dictionary of Samala in 1972, and he has been working on it ever since; the beautifully produced Samala/English dictionary is the culmination of his work. As the tribe says in the introduction, "With this guide to our language, we not only provide you with a glimpse into a language that is as fascinating as it is complex, we also provide an opportunity to see how our ancestors lived" (Santa Ynez Band of Chumash Indians and Applegate, 2007:5).

p. 114 *As we saw above...* The quote "most of what we know today about the Samala language and a great deal of what we know of the culture has been preserved because of Maria Solares's willingness to share her knowledge with Harrington" is from Applegate (2007:11). The quote that Maria's father's parents came "from Kalawashaq, the second-largest village in Ineseño territory" is from Applegate (2007:10). See also Robinson 2009.

p. 114 *Solares, then, is central to the tribe's history and heritage.* In 2007, Nakia Zavalla, the cultural programs director, and the other language apprentices, were approached by the elders to put together a celebration of Maria Solares on her birthday, April 15. Nakia turns wistful and quiet when I ask her about the celebration. "She is my great-great-great-grandmother, and it meant a lot to me. I am really starting to get to know her more intimately and really not just as informant but as my grandmother and making that personal connection with her. To be asked by the elders was huge. I do not take it lightly. How do we honor a woman that has left us all that we know about our language and traditional ways, everything we have?" The dinner was provided by a descendant, an education funds beneficiary who attended culinary school. Another descendant who graduated from an art institute in Pasadena drew the beautiful painting of Maria Solares. Joe Talaugon, who was the chair of the Elders Committee when I interviewed him, says that such ceremonies are important for the elders, many of whom discovered or rediscovered their Chumash identity late in life. "Knowing a little bit more about your ancestors, how they lived and what they believed, opens up a lot of the present-day elders to be more aware of this spirituality. When you open up to Indian spirituality, you open up to a whole new world."

p. 116   *There are currently revitalization movements in other Chumash groups...* Coastal and valley Chumash have also cooperated in establishing demonstration villages in state parks and museums (such as at Jalama State Beach Park and the Santa Barbara Museum of Natural History) and in welcoming indigenous Maya activist and Nobel Laureate Rigoberta Menchu to Chumash territory. These and other cultural projects are bringing Chumash peoples together in new ways that work in favor of their cultural identities. Kathy Marshall says that although sometimes there have been resentment and tension among different groups, there is also solidarity. "We [Samala Chumash] are different because we are federally recognized, and that does cause a bit of separation. But we're also Indians, we're Chumash, and we're all here doing the same thing, trying to protect our culture and trying to teach our children our culture. And that's more important than anything else." Another striking example of the ways that the casino revenues have supported pan-Indian solidarity is the assembly bill that was signed into law in 2009. While the issue of teacher credentialing in California native languages was brought up by native groups from northern California, "the Santa Ynez Band of Chumash Indians, a tribe with gaming resources, stepped up to press for legislation" (*LAT*, 2/7/13). The new law "requires the California Commission on Teacher Credentialing to issue an 'American Indian languages credential' to teachers recommended by federally recognized tribes that are authorized to establish their own fluency tests" (*LAT*, 2/7/13). This new law has had a positive impact on linguistic and cultural revitalization among several California tribes, including the largest tribe in California, the Yurok of northern California.

p. 117   *Another important venue for intertribal solidarity and cultural revitalization is the tomol crossing…* Reggie emphasizes that it is not just about the crossing, but about generating community. "While the paddlers carry prayers for family members as they cross, the tomol is just the cog in the wheel; it creates the spiritual bond that brings us together." The island camp becomes a small village that is inclusive, according to Reggie. "There's natives and non-natives, families, friends, and supporters. There's no color barrier, no race barrier. We sing Indian songs as well as doo-wop! 'You are part of us'—for three days,'" he tells me. "There are more tears leaving the island because you've just left a whole community of people that are there—the tomol is just a part of it, a small part of it. As much as I love her [the tomol], I know she's very small in the big picture. She's integral, but in the big picture you're talking people's lives and how they identify with themselves, with their culture, and that's huge. I mean you make an impact on a life and I think that all us of want to do something. I am happy to say I have helped native people reidentify themselves."

p. 118   *The trip itself is hazardous.* A major hazard that the Chumash in pre-colonial times did not have to deal with is large container ships. In the channel there are two main shipping lanes, each a mile wide with a mile wide gap between them. "What we have to do is get across between the large freighters that are seven football fields long with cargo; they've got a swell buster that's ten by ten coming off the front of it to make sure they can go through without any problems in the water. And we're only thirty feet long and that makes it rather interesting navigation," Reggie Pagaling says, laughing. "We have support boats around us to help us with that but these guys are traveling at twenty-five to forty knots in the water and we're going three or four, so our timing has to be perfect to get across. We have to know that they are fifteen miles away or we'll hold up." Sharing prayers and celebrating a difficult journey together, the channel crossing is a powerful event for those involved. This new tradition, reviving a central Chumash practice that died over a hundred and fifty years ago, is a rite of passage for several younger Chumash each year. As one high school student put it, "I'm not just a junior paddler anymore. I'm an actual paddler now. I'm doing what my ancestors were doing thousands of years ago" (*LAT*, 9/21/04).

p. 119   *The Annual Chumash Intertribal Pow Wow is an excellent example of how the casino revenues enhance solidarity…* The pow wows of the '60s and '70s were modest in scope.

As Kathy Marshall remembers, "We used to make the *ramadas* ourselves and if you had a booth, it was just a table and a chair, and I think there was just one food vendor selling food. It was tiny." The annual intertribal pow wows hosted by the tribe since the mid-'90s have grown greatly in size, and more and more native and non-native people are attending them each year.

p. 120   *The Chumash are promoting intertribal solidarity in other ways...* Armenta's quote, "I don't believe I've ever been caught speechless" is taken from the *SBNP* (12/23/04). Adelina has also represented her people and given prayer at intertribal and indigenous women's rights meetings in New York, Texas, Minnesota, Montana, Washington DC, and throughout California. She has also represented her people at forums in Canada, Mexico, Panama, and South Africa. In all these places, she uses her personal casino revenues to help people. As she puts it, "With the casino revenues I've been able to put legs on a young girl in Mexico. I was able to send a young man to trade school in South Africa. I'm able to help the Cuna people from Panama, to help this little [Cuna] boy get his kidney out."

p. 120   *In the different instances and levels of cultural revitalization...* As someone who, under the leadership of the late Dr. Fred Loveys, helped found this program and who taught in it for three summers, I can speak firsthand of the way the program has changed over the years. It has gone from serving a handful of students, having a largely non-Chumash staff, and being run through the Education Department to being a large, well-established program run by the cultural programs director and by a good number of engaged Chumash adults. Until the summer of 2007, the camp was based at the Sedgwick Reserve of UCSB, a sprawling and beautiful piece of wilderness used for scientific research. Some of the docents there gave lectures on the surrounding ecology. During each summer, we camped for several days on Santa Cruz Island, with several dozen Chumash participants—youth, mentors, and family members. Several Chumash parents and other Native Americans who had married into the tribe contributed with stories and games. A professional storyteller from the coastal Chumash also participated. Prayer and talking circles usually marked the beginning and end of each day, and even the most rowdy Chumash kids respect talking circles, prayer, and other ceremony. At present some of the kids from the original summer program have become youth mentors, and today at Camp Kalawashaq it is clear that younger students are getting the message that "it is cool to respect the culture," as one of the adult mentors tells me. Another one adds, "It builds self-esteem and teaches them respect for the elders."

Seven   Cultural Power

Epigram is from an interview the author conducted with Joe Talaugon.

p. 137   *Some Chumash individuals are also researching and rewriting history themselves.*
After graduating from high school and serving in the Korean War, Talaugon became a
sheet metal worker. Both he and his wife became political activists, doing community
work around issues of discrimination in the workplace in the San Francisco area and
elsewhere in California. He also got involved in civil rights marches, visited reservations, and was even involved with the American Indian Movement. After an amazing
coincidence and a lot of historical research, Joe found out the truth about his past.
One of Joe's daughters was working on the Chumash reservation as a census taker in
1970. "So, she was out there at Santa Ynez and she starts talking to this one lady who
asks her who her grandmother was. She calls me up and says, 'You know, Dad, there's
a lot of relatives all over here. You have to come down here.' I said, 'Really?' 'Yeah,
Grandma has relatives.' They remembered my mom when she was a little girl and her
mother. Once we found out who was who with these relatives, I came down immediately to meet some of them. This was '70, '71, '72. So I would come down often and
they would say, 'Yes, your grandma this and that.'"

p. 138   *Joe grows reflective as he discusses this important transformation in his life.* The
culmination of Joe's transformation came during a spiritual ceremony in Northern
California in 1989. This is when he "felt the connection to the Great Spirit" and
decided to dedicate himself to Native American cultural and political issues. The
ceremony was led by a Wintu American Indian lady on Mount Shasta in northern
California. First she prayed and did ceremony and then, out of a crowd of over two
hundred people she picked five people, one of whom was Joe Talaugon, to address the
crowd. He recounts, "She didn't know me, I didn't know her. So I says, 'Why me?'
She says, 'You're an older person and you're a spiritual person.' I said, 'No, I'm not,
I'm not a spiritual person.' She said, 'No, you come up here, I want you here anyway.'
So I went up there and stood, and up to that time I had no knowledge or feeling of
what it means to be spiritually connected, because I was raised as a Catholic, but I
hadn't continued as Catholic. I had dropped away from the church because of all the
things I learned. But that night, she said, 'You have to speak to the people, you have
to throw your heart out, you have to tell everything that you have inside,' and I did.
I got up there—and it was in a big meadow with trees all around, it was dark—and I
was speaking about things from my soul and my heart that was bothering me through
the years. Such as my mother denying me so much knowledge, my upbringing, a lot

198

of things that I wondered about, my identity. 'Who am I? Who am I? Where do I come from?' So all this came off that night when I found out who I was. I didn't see a vision but I could feel the connection to the Great Spirit. From that time on, I told them, I am going to dedicate the rest of my life to whatever I feel like doing, and this cultural center is part of it. You run into problems, but you keep on going. That's my mission, I have to do this."

p. 140   *Joe is not the only tribal member who thinks it should be the Chumash themselves...* The quote by Sandoval is from Sandoval (2007:45).

Eight   Critique and Rebuttal

In the epigram, the quote by Richard Gomez is from the *SYVN* (10/12/06).

p. 150   *Those who lead the opposition to the Chumash are for the most part wealthy local citizens.* The Concerned Citizens group formed in 1997 and for a long time was led by a man whose family has long owned a nearby "guest ranch," with a hotel, two golf courses, and restaurants. Some candidates for local positions of power, such as one man who ran for county supervisor in 2008, are active in these groups and have often run on thinly veiled "anti-Chumash" tickets. The local weekly, *The Valley Journal*, has, since its inception, consistently attacked the tribe. Celebrity residents who have spoken out against the tribe include Bo Derek, David Crosby, Doc Severinsen, and Bernie Taupin. Together, this relatively small but vocal group of ranchers, celebrities, and others—some from the left but mostly from the right—have mobilized opposition to the Chumash. The local papers, the *Santa Ynez Valley News*, the *Santa Ynez Valley Journal*, and the *Santa Barbara News Press*, with their editorials, letters to the editor, and even advertisements from opposing groups, are a fount of information about these opposition groups, the response of Chumash supporters, as well as about local culture and politics in general.

p. 150   *This is exemplified by the writings of the most outspoken...* For me, it is surprising that this "progressive rocker" and countercultural icon would insult the tribe in his book, *Since Then* (2006). Although a generous supporter of local arts programs in the valley, Crosby shows a studied ignorance of local history and the non-elite local community. In a more recent, 2009 interview, Crosby's rhetoric toward the tribe has mellowed (*SYVJ*, Dec. 24–25, 2009). Among other things, he does not make personal attacks against the tribe, admits that he plays concerts at other Indian casinos, and states that he is not against the tribe having a casino. Yet Crosby continues to say that he does not believe "that the tribes are a separate entity. I don't believe they should be and I don't believe they are" (*SYVJ*, Dec. 24–25, 2009:9). Again, American Indians in federally recognized tribes are legally dual citizens, whether Crosby believes it or not, and the fact is that this was not engineered by the tribes but by the government of the United States. Despite such statements, it is clear that Crosby has reconsidered some of his stronger words against his neighbors in the valley. He recently was honored at a 2010 local school fundraiser for his contributions to the arts of the valley, and this fundraiser was held at the Chumash's Hotel Corque and catered by the celebrity chef hired by the tribe for their fine-dining restaurant, Root 246.

p. 150   *According to local writer William Etling...* As Etling notes at the end of his book, back in 1977 there was already much debate over developing the valley. The quote "The hot button has never been who's doing the developing..." is from Etling (2005:274). The quote "A resident since 1966, I'm hard pressed to remember any development plan that wasn't opposed by somebody. Local preservationists are equal opportunity developer bashers" is from Etling (2005:275). Etling, a local writer who for many years had a "Valley Sketchbook" column in the *Valley News*, compiled a number of his articles in a book, *Sideways in Neverland* (2005). His short thematic essays sketch the cowboys and local ranching culture, Danish heritage, local celebrities and artists, and the burgeoning wine industry. See also Firestone (2010).

p. 151   *But, in fact, the Chumash are treated very differently...* Not only the tone but also many of the criticisms made of the tribe are very different from those leveled at other potential developers. The president of POLO declared that "POLO does not support any restrictions on wine tasting rooms." The quote that tasting rooms are "good for agriculture" is taken from the *SYVJ* (Sept. 24–30, 2009). Equal opportunity development basher POLO is not.

p. 151   *Another example of the double standard of the most aggressive adversaries...* The quote "In that case, I think that they, POLO should change their name to something other than Preservation of Los Olivos" is from a letter to the editor in the *Valley Journal* (December 11–17, 2008:13). To provide a little more background, a local group, the Valley Alliance, nominated Matteis for historical landmark status. The new owners and developers of Matteis opposed it, saying it had been done without their consent and that it would inhibit the scope of their development. They said that they would get Matteis landmarked once their project was completed. The private property reasons cited by POLO for opposing landmark recognition are found in the *SYVN* (3/11/2010). After first stating at a town hall meeting in Los Olivos in September of 2009 (*SYVJ*: Sept. 24–30, 2009) that they would not contest the development, they came out as one of its most vocal proponents. Full-page ads taken out in both the *Valley Journal* and the *Valley News* by a group calling itself "In Defense of Property Rights" took the argument even further: "It is possible that you may lose control of the right to protect your private property and to have fair and equitable treatment in Santa Barbara County unless the Santa Barbara Historic Landmark Advisory Commission (HLAC) members reconsider their May 10th vote to landmark private property without the owner's consent... If the members approve this nomination, your property may be significantly devalued" (*SYVN* June 15, 2010). The editorials and letters to the editor about the Matteis controversy were revealing. The president of the Valley Alliance spoke of the public good, saying "Land marking is inherently an open public process and nomination for Historical Landmark status should have come as no surprise to the developer—the Historic Landmarks Advisory Commission first suggested it in 1982...the scale and intensity of what was proposed was cause for concern... The landmark process allows members of the public to nominate historic properties for landmark status. To not do so in this case would have been to turn our back on our own Valley history, our own Matteis Tavern" (*SYVN* Feb. 18, 2010). Another local resident stated in his letter to the editor, "We do not wish to have the last stagecoach stop in California altered or destroyed so a large hotel complex can be built to house wine business customers... the idea of destroying an early California landmark doesn't fly well with me and a lot of other residents. We are not tourists. We live here and work here. This is our Valley and we have something to say" (*SYVN* January 21, 2010). Another letter writer was equally outspoken: "We do not need a high-dollar, chi-chi monstrosity catering to the wine and haute cuisine crowd, and we sure don't need to trash what is a historic treasure to create it..." (*SYVJ*: Jan. 28–Feb. 3 2010). Clearly, although POLO asserts that it represents "the community," it in fact represents the particular interests of a much smaller group.

p. 152 *Pseudo experts or "historical consultants" have been hired.* For the 2012 article by this "expert," see *SYVN* (3/15/12). Besides the fact that old censuses are notoriously unreliable, the articles are riddled with misinformation and selective in their reading.

p. 152 *A week later, John Johnson...* The quote by Johnson, "there is no question..." comes from *SYVN* (3/22/12). He continues, "María Solares' parents, grandparents and great-grandparents were all baptized at Mission Santa Inés... Mr. Lynch obviously never examined any church records for the Santa Ynez tribe, or he would not have made the false statement that María Solares was not a tribal member... Her three marriages and all of her children's baptisms are also recorded in church records. María and her parents were listed in the first census made of the Indians living at Zanja de Cota in 1856, and she continued to live in the Santa Ynez tribal community for her entire life." The parents of her father-in-law, Rafael Solares, had come from the large valley village of Soxtonokmu. Maria Solares's parents on her father's side came from Kalawashaq (Applegate 2007:10). In his 2006 book, David Crosby also supported the idea that the Chumash are not authentic. "The danger is that what we're dealing with here is not so much a tribe as a single family that controls a gang. And frankly, if you want to see them blanch and then get really mad, start talking about DNA testing for who's really an Indian and who isn't. If the guy who's running the tribe here has any Indian blood in him at all, it's a miracle" (Crosby 2006:244).

p. 152   *Not just scholars but local residents...* The quote "the consistent claim that any tribe cannot be 'real' Indians" is from a guest editorial in the *Valley Journal* (August 6–12, 2009:15). The author continues, "The anti Indian argument gets a bit confusing when it makes statements such as 'anyone can claim to be part Indian' and then attacks the Santa Ynez for having enrollment standards in the same breath. Whether or not you agree with the enrollment criteria, it is not true that 'just anyone' can sign up to be part of the band." The writer suggests that the "bashers of the Santa Ynez Band should just canter back to the 1830s, when Chief Justice Marshall ruled that native tribes are 'domestic dependent nations'.... Like any other nation, they have the right to set the standards for who can be a citizen of their nation. Ergo, the federal government will usually not get involved any more than it would in the citizenships laws of England or France." The author continues, "It is more likely one will seeing pigs flying in formation over the mission than witness the federal government interfering with a functioning, self-sufficient native nation that also contributes to the surrounding community in spite of all the abuse that it has suffered in the past at their hands."

p. 153   *David Crosby in* Since Then *says...* The quote "Ask the people who live around the casino" is from Crosby (2006:242).

p. 153   *The tribe has been an excellent neighbor.* This quote is from "The Sustainable Chumash: Inside the Santa Ynez Band of Mission Indians' Quest to Go Green." *SBI* (5/24/12). The article goes on to document the many ways that the Chumash are applying green technologies in the casino and throughout the reservation.

p. 154   *The Chumash also give a lot back to the community*. Many of the Chumash individuals that I interviewed spoke of the great satisfaction that they feel in regard to the tribe helping out organizations that used to help tribal members is times of need.

p. 154   *But Chumash generosity extends far past the organizations that helped them in the past*. The list of donations includes a $1-million-dollar donation to the Santa Ynez Valley Cottage Hospital (*SYVJ* May 11–18, 2007). The information of donations to the Blackfeet Reservation and one hundred thousand dollars for Hurricane Katrina and Hurricane Rita victims comes from the *SYVN* (10/8/2009).

p. 154   *According to Crosby...* The information for the arrests/offense report comes from the *SYVJ* (June 17-23, 2010). The police blotter in the local newspapers contains weekly reports of crime, and a significant amount of it takes place in or around the casino.

p. 155   *Crosby asserts that the casinos...* The quote "say they put money into local economies but the truth is that almost of it goes out of town, out of state and offshore" is from Crosby (2006:242).

p. 155   *A 2008 economic study funded by...* This report does not take a stand on the issue of gambling or its expansion in California and does not address the social impact of the casino. As the executive director of the association says, "There are positive and negative impacts associated with every economic entity in Santa Barbara County. The bigger the entity, the more the impact, positive and negative.... [The casino is] throwing off a lot of economic activity and economic value. We wanted to know how much" (*SBNP* Feb. 26, 08). Among its other findings, the report found that the casino has one of the largest direct payrolls in the county, and, for all workers, pays salaries higher on average than the average salaries earned by all workers in Santa Barbara County. The tribe offers a wide variety of jobs and the possibility of career advancement. I would add that the many Chumash descendants attending universities and colleges are contributing to the skilled labor force of the county and beyond.

p. 155   *The casino also contributes to government tax revenue and to the income of local businesses.* "The respending by Chumash Casino employees is a significant economic driver resulting in $58 million in additional sales and $14 million in tax payments to the government" (*SBNP*, Feb. 26, 2008).

p. 156 *As we saw above, the Chumash have donated...* The quote about a state-mandated process "to help local governments handle off-reservation impacts of tribal gaming" is from the *SYVN* (March 6, 2007).

p. 156 *All these contributions and the local economic impact of the Chumash, however, are downplayed...* The *Valley Journal*, for example, published a series of articles in 2010 that maintained that Chumash contributions do not begin to match the tax revenues needed for local services and infrastructure. The revenues are lost, one article claimed, because the Chumash tribal members and the casino do not pay property taxes or income taxes. He also asserted that these missing monies have to be made up by non-Indian taxpayers and that "there is little benefit to any of the surrounding businesses" (*SYVJ* June 24–28, 2010).

p. 156 *Many locals beg to differ.* This letter writer says that she is not a gambler but finds the casino a fantastic venue for entertainment and fine dining (*SYVJ* June 17-23, 2010).

p. 157 *Implicit in the Chumash opponents' arguments is that American Indians somehow invented...* Crosby (2006:244) further states: "I know they had a rough time of it, but so did the Irish and the blacks. That was then, this is now. None of the punks that are running the casino were at Wounded Knee and neither was I." Although this country was founded on noble ideals, it was not until the later twentieth century that women and different peoples of color, including Native Americans, actually participated in those ideals and civil rights. Reservations were a form of forced segregation, and, in the case of Santa Ynez, until the early 1970s tribal residents did not have the basic services of electricity, water, and gas that the rest of the valley population enjoyed. Another common misconception exemplified in Crosby's words is that Native American tribes are just like the "Irish and the blacks," that is, like other minority groups that have suffered, rather than having the particularity of being native to this land and having been recognized as preexisting, self-governing nations by invading colonists. Again, American Indians did not invent this system.

p. 157 *As we saw earlier in this book...* For the important role that American Indians have played in the United States military, see Robinson 2008b, 2008c.

p. 157 *Crosby, voicing a common misconception...* The quote "use our schools, roads, hospitals, firemen, and police, and they don't pay taxes" is taken from Crosby (2006:242).

p. 158   *A topic of much debate is the "fee-to-trust" process...* The late Fess Parker, an actor who famously played Disney's Davy Crockett for many years before settling in the valley and becoming a winemaker and major developer, allied himself with the Chumash in 2004 to carry out this project. Because of fierce opposition, the proposal was eventually scuttled by the tribe (see Etling 2005:87-103). However, in 2010, just a few days after Fess Parker's death, it was revealed that the tribe had purchased fourteen hundred acres of land from him before his death. There is heated debate about the future of this land in local newspapers and in large forums organized by the Chumash and by their opponents.

p. 158   *We find "the community" narrowly defined...* The arguments of the tribal opponents ignore a large portion of the population. Once one gets to know the Chumash and their descendants, one spots them everywhere around town. Chumash youth work in local stores and eateries; other Chumash have businesses, and Chumash descendants are recognized as competitive athletes at the local high school. Today, more and more Chumash kids can be found in the private schools of the valley. But what of the Latino population, with which Chumash individuals are often confused? As we saw previously, Mexicans have lived in the Valley for over one hundred and eighty years, and the Chumash have long been tied to this population. Since the 1980s, there has been a large influx of Mexicans and other Latinos, and their numbers are growing. They come looking for a better life and the great majority work hard and confront many challenges to achieve it. Many families who originally arrived as illegal migrants in the '80s and '90s now are US residents and citizens, have their own businesses, and own expensive residences in the valley. However, many of the local Latinos are relatively recent migrants, and they are often in the country illegally. They are part of the urban and rural poor of the valley. They work largely in restaurants, hotels, as ranch hands and farm workers, as domestics and landscapers. Until the casino brought jobs and wealth to the Chumash and their descendants, they were a largely indistinguishable part of this "Latino" workforce. The rural workforce on ranches and vineyards is made up largely of Mexicans who come from the rural regions of Oaxaca, Michoacán, Guerrero, and Jalisco. Although many ranches and vineyards treat their workers well, others do not. Substandard housing with only cold water, exposure to pesticides in the fields, and low wages are just some of the conditions that many farm and ranch workers and their families have to face. As illegal migrants, they are vulnerable to having their cars impounded, and they themselves are vulnerable to being caught in *redadas* and deported. What is not acknowledged by those who would not include this group of people in "the community" is how dependent our community is on them. While often denigrated as "unskilled labor," most farm workers bring extensive knowledge about farming and ranching. To a large degree, this rural Mexican knowledge and know-how underwrites the success of many ranches and vineyards. In this important way, farm workers also form part of the valley community, whether the opponents of the Chumash count them or not. And woe to those members of our community who are the "undocumented laborers" and "illegals," who work in the Danish restaurants in Solvang, on the farms and vineyards throughout the valley, who clean the homes and care for the children of their more affluent valley neighbors. Not only are they vulnerable in the work place and on the streets, but many valley residents would vote to have their children denied education or access to health care. Not only are they criminalized for just trying to make a living and support their families but are the object of scorn from the dominant society. In between articles, commentaries, and letters critiquing the tribe, one also finds many anti-immigrant letters in the conservative and Chumash-bashing *Valley Journal*. One letter writer (*SYVJ* Apr. 3–8, 2008) says, "I cannot imagine one country in the world willing to endanger every law abiding citizen to all disease by looking the other way when illegal aliens come and go at will spreading disease. Our silence on this issue is subjecting our children to pain, suffering, expense, crippling debilitation, and even death due to foreign diseases such as hepatitis, tuberculosis, human rabies, and measles to name a few." Another letter writer is even more extreme: "The illegal aliens and anchor babies are trying to out-populate the Americans and put their own in power. The liberals do nothing because they are pandering for future votes" (*SYVJ* Jan. 14–20, 2010).

Nine   Moving Toward Understanding and Reconciliation

The epigrams from this chapter are taken from Crosby (2006:244) and *SYVN* (3/8/2007), respectively.

p. 162   *The preceding chapters suggest an alternative view of history and society in this region of rural California.* Besides the cultural diversity presented found beneath the surface, my alternative view also shows that there is economic diversity. All the valley's sub-cultures (white, Chumash, Latino) have class divisions. Behind the beautiful valley scenes along country roads and in and around the country towns and Danish village, there is often hidden poverty. People Helping People, a local nonprofit dedicated to assisting low-income people in the valley, has its hands full. Although in fact the poor in the valley include almost all ethnic groups, a large percentage are Latino, first- or second-generation migrants generally from Mexico, who do the menial jobs and farm work. This is the same work that many Chumash did before the casino.

p. 166   *As far as bridging differences with regard to education...* The quote "all participants must acknowledge" is from Sandoval (2007:101). Sandoval goes on to offer a number of suggestions for reconciling tensions within the education system and for advancing the education of not just the Chumash but all students in the valley through collaboration among tribal officials, educational researchers, parents, and educators. There is a need to develop curricular materials and professional development opportunities for teachers to learn about local history and the native inhabitants of the land, as well as to have native culture-bearers work on site. Teaching all students about the indigenous knowledge systems that have existed in this area for millennia can inform disciplines as diverse as astronomy and biology to language arts, mathematics, and environmental science, and this "enriches the learning experience for all students" (Ibid:103).

p. 167   *The Santa Ynez Chumash tribe is just one native community among thousands and thousands throughout the Americas...* The potential for casino tribes to contribute to the educational and cultural initiatives of non-recognized tribes and to indigenous communities throughout the Americas is great. As one comprehensive review of the current state of Native Nations declares, "Native nations today are in key respects like other emergent and reemergent nations in the world. They are trying to do everything at once—self-govern effectively, build economies, improve social conditions, and strengthen culture and identity" (Harvard Project on American Indian Economic Development 2008:13). While the net proceeds of the billions of dollars being generated by tribal casinos across the country are dedicated to tribal government operations, economic development, and charitable organizations, a significant amount also finds its way to culture and education. As Sandoval notes, "Education programs generated by native communities, dedicated to the transmission of indigenous knowledge including language, science, and technology, are now implemented on an unprecedented scale. Tribal investment in education is accelerating rapidly, fueling community revitalization" (2007:4). Shrewd investment by casino tribes have the potential of not only leading to greater economic self-determination of indigenous peoples throughout the Americas but also to changing the pervasive cultural politics and educational systems that continue to marginalize indigenous identity and limit social mobility.

Acknowledgments

This book would not have been possible without the kind help of many people. In particular, I would like to offer my sincere thanks to the Santa Ynez Chumash Elders Committee and Education Committee; Adelina Alva-Padilla, the spiritual leader of the tribe; Nakia Zavalla, the cultural programs director and language apprentice, and her brother, Desi Zavalla; William Wyatt, formerly the Environmental Department director and now the tribal administrator; Freddy Romero, cultural preservation consultant and tribal liaison with various government agencies; Reggie Pagaling and Tom Lopez, tomol paddlers; Niki Sandoval, the education programs director; the elders, including Tonie "Chuca" Flores, Dolores Cross, Esther Manguray, and Joe Talaugon, who is also the founder of Guadalupe Cultural Arts and Education Center; Frances Snyder, formerly the Chumash public relations executive director; Carmen Sandoval, Tom Lopez, and Kathy Marshall, language apprentices; Pete Crowheart Zavalla, Tribal Relations Program manager for the Forest Service; Richard Applegate, the director of the Chumash Language Program; Leslie Koda, the former director of the American Indian Scholars Program at UCSB; Kathleen Conti, director of Museum Programs, Research, and Resources; and John Johnson, curator of Anthropology at the Santa Barbara Museum of Natural History.

Conversations with Ben Munger, Jacob Grant, Greg Donovan, Tharon Weighill, and Kate Spilde have taught me much. The work of Gary Robinson and our talks through the years have been especially illuminating, and I am grateful for his vast knowledge of native America. I would like to give special thanks to him and Dolores Cross, Tonie Flores and Secondino Flores, and Adelina Alva-Padilla and Osvaldo Casillas, and to their extended families, for their friendship and generosity of spirit.

The idea for this book originated while I was working in the Chumash summer program during the summers of 2003, 2004, and 2005. This was a wonderful learning experience for me, and I would like to give many thanks to the students of those years, who are now much taller and much older. My appreciation also extends to the Sedgwick Reserve, which hosted the camp, and to the late Fred Loveys, Sarah Moses, Dominica Valencia, Jonathan Kim, Larry Madrigal, and the many others involved in the program, for the teaching, learning, and camaraderie of those years.

Summer research grants were provided by California Nations Indian Gaming Association through the Center for California Native Nations at the University of California at Riverside in 2005, and by the Sycuan Institute for Tribal Gaming in 2007 and 2008. I would like to send the institute and Kate Spilde special thanks. I would also like to thank Will Graham and my colleagues at Midland School for the 2009 Faculty Lecture Award and the chance to present my research to the student body.

Paul Roberts, a graduate student at UC Riverside, provided invaluable research assistance in the summer of 2005. Andrew Hurley, a student at Midland School, assisted me in 2007 and 2008. I would like to thank these individuals and also Emma Munger for the wonderful maps, drawing, and cover design that she contributed to this book. I am also grateful to the National Anthropological Archives of the Smithsonian Institution, and to the Santa Ynez Historical Society and Curt Cragg, for the historical photographs. I learned a great deal discussing photos with Curt and I would like to send a special thanks to him for his help. So, too, many thanks go to Joe Talaugon, Tonie Flores, William Wyatt, and Gary Robinson for allowing me to use their photos.

The skillful editing of Pamela Fischer and the incisive comments offered by Niki Sandoval, Orin Starn, Eric Deeds, Harry P. Gelles, and Matthew Bokovoy on previous drafts made this a better book. Very special thanks go out to Eric Deeds, who created the index and whose keen eye for detail helped this book in too many ways to mention. Thanks Eric. This book has also benefited from comments offered by anonymous reviewers for Heyday Press, the University of Nebraska Press, Oxford University Press, and the University of New Mexico Press. Nonetheless, the option of self-publishing now allows one to dispense with the politics and glacial pace of academic publishing, and I would like to thank Carina, Andrea, and the rest of the staff at CreateSpace for assisting me in the production of this book.

My interest in indigenous people was greatly stimulated by the late David Maybury-Lewis, wonderful friend and teacher, and by his wife, Pia. To them and to all of the above-mentioned individuals and institutions, many, many thanks.

Finally, to my wife, Iliana, for her constant support and patience during the writing of this book, and to my children Daniela and Darien for their welcome distractions, I send my deepest gratitude and love.

Bibliography

Newspapers
LAT	*Los Angeles Times*
SMT	*Santa Maria Times*
SYVN	*Santa Ynez Valley News*
SBNP	*Santa Barbara News Press*
SYVJ	*Santa Ynez Valley Journal*
SBI	*Santa Barbara Independent*

Alexie, Sherman
2007   *The Absolutely True Diary of a Part-Time Indian.* Little, Brown and Company.

Anderson, Benedict
1983   *Imagined Communities.* London: Verso.

Applegate, Richard
n.d.   unpublished manuscript
1972   "Ineseño Chumash Grammar." Ph.D. Dissertation, University of California at Berkeley.
1975a   "An Index of Chumash Place Names." *Papers on the Chumash.* Occasional Paper Number 9, San Luis Obispo County Archeological Society, Pp. 19-46.
1975b   "The Datura Cult among the Chumash. *Journal of California Anthropology.* 2 (1):7-17.
2007   "Introduction." In *Samala-English Dictionary.* Santa Ynez Band of Chumash Indians in Collaboration with Richard Applegate.

Blackburn, Thomas
1975   *Decembers Child: A Book of Chumash Oral Narratives.*
               University of California Press.

Black Gold Cooperative Library System in Collaboration with John Johnson
1997   *Native Americans on the Central Coast: A Photo Essay Depicting
               Aspects of the Life of the Native American Community in the
               Counties of San Luis Obispo, Santa Barbara, and Ventura.* Black
               Gold Cooperative.

California State Department of Education
1931   "Survey of School Conditions in Santa Ynez Union High
               School District."

Cattelino, Jessica R.
2008   *High Stakes: Florida Seminole Gaming and Sovereignty.* Duke
               University Press.

Cooper
1999   *Indian School: Teaching the White Man's Way.* Clarion Books.

Cragg, Curt
2006   *Buellton.* Arcadia Publishing.

2008   *Solvang.* Arcadia Publishing.

Cramer, Renee Ann
2005   *Cash, Color, and Colonialism: The Politics of Tribal
               Acknowledgment.* University of Oklahoma Press.

Crosby, David
2006   *Since Then: How I Survived Everything and Lived to Tell About
               It.* Putnam and Sons.

Dana, Richard Henry
1986   *Two Years before the Mast.* Penguin Books.

Darian-Smith, Eve
2004   *New Capitalists: Law, Politics, and Identity Surrounding Casino
                Gaming on Native American Land.* Wadsworth.

Easton, Ellen and Bjorn Rye
1996   *Ranchos. Santa Barbara Land Grant Ranches.* Easton Gallery.

Etling, William
2005   *Sideways in Neverland. Life in the Santa Ynez Valley, California.*
                iUniverse.

Faulkner, William
1950   *Requiem for a Nun.* Vintage.

Firestone, Brooks
2010   *Valley Animals: True Stories about the Animals and People of
                California's Santa Ynez Valley.* Fithian Press.

Gamble, Lynn H.
2008   *The Chumash World at European Contact: Power, Trade, and Feasting
                Among Complex Hunter-Gatherers.* University of California Press.

Gardner, Leigh, J.P. Kalt, and Katherine A. Spilde
2005   *Annotated Bibliography: The Social and Economic Impacts of
                Indian and Other Gaming.* Harvard Project on American
                Indian Economic Development.

Gardner, Louise
1965   "The Surviving Chumash." Archeological Survey Annual
                Report (Los Angeles) 7:277-302.

Geertz, Clifford
1998   "Deep Hanging Out." *The New York Review of Books* 45
                (16):69-72.

Gelles, Paul H.
1990   "Latin America's Indian Question," with David Maybury-
                Lewis. *The Wilson Quarterly*, Washington DC, 14 (3): 58-60.

1995   "Equilibrium and Extraction: Dual Organization in the
            Andes." *American Ethnologist* 22 (4): 710-742.
1996   "Introduction." *Andean Lives: Gregorio Condori Mamana and
            Asunta Quispe Huaman.* Ricardo Valderrama and Carmen
            Escalante, editors. Pp.1-13. University of Texas Press.
1998   "Indigenous Peoples and Their Conquests." *American
            Anthropologist.* Vol. 98(2):408-411.
2000   *Water and Power in Highland Peru: The Cultural Politics of
            Irrigation and Development.* Rutgers University Press.
2002   "Andean Culture, Indigenous Identity, and the State in
            Peru." In *The Politics of Ethnicity: Indigenous Peoples in Latin
            American States.* David Maybury-Lewis, editor. Pp.278-301.
            Cambridge: Harvard University Press.
2005a   "Education and Culture: The Impact of the Casino on the
            Santa Ynez Chumash." Report for the Center for California
            Native Nations, University of California at Riverside.
2005b   "Transformaciones en una comunidad andina transnacio-
            nal." In *El Quinto Suyo.* Ulla Berg and Karsten Paerregaard,
            editors. Pp.69-96. Instituto de Estudios Peruanos.

Grant, Campbell
1967   *Rock Art of the American Indian.* Dillon, Co.: Vista Books.

Harvard Project on American Indian Economic Development
2008   *The State of the Native Nations.* Oxford University Press.

Haley, Brian and Larry Wilcoxon
1997   "Anthropology and the Making of Chumash Tradition."
            Current Anthropology 38(5):761-794.

Holmes, Marie S. and John R. Johnson
1998   *The Chumash and their Predecessors: An Annotated Bibliography.*
            Santa Barbara Museum of Natural History.

Hudson, Travis, editor.
1979   *Breath of the Sun. Life in Early California As Told by a
            Chumash Indian, Fernando Librado to John P. Harrington.*
            Malki Museum Press.

Hudson, Travis
1980   "The Chumash Revolt of 1824. Another Native Account from the Notes of John P. Harrington." *Journal of California and Great Basin Anthropology* 2(1):231-126.

Hudson, Travis and Thomas Blackburn, Rosario Curletti, and Janice Timbrook, eds.
1981   *The Eye of the Flute. Chumash Traditional History and Ritual As Told by Fernando Librado Kitsepawit to John P. Harrington.* Malki Museum Press.

Hudson, Travis and Ernest Underhay
1978   *Crystals in the Sky: An Intellectual Odyssey Involving Chumash Astronomy, Cosmology, and Rock Art.* Ballena Press.

Isaacson, Robert and Tom Moore, eds.
2004   *Cattle upon a Thousand Hills: Ranch Life in Santa Barbara County in the Twentieth Century as Recorded in Family Albums.* Bagaduce Press.

Johnson, John
1984   "Indian History in the Santa Barbara Back Country." In Los Padres Notes, Volume 3. Los Padres Interpretive Association.
1988   *Chumash Social Organization.* Unpublished PhD dissertation. University of California at Santa Barbara.
1989   "The Chumash and the Missions." In *Archeological and Historical Perspectives on the Spanish Borderlands West.* Smithsonian Institution Press.
1990   "The Chumash Indians After Secularization." Selected Paper and Commentaries from the November 1990 Quincentenary Symposium.
1994   "Chumash." In *Native America in the Twentieth Century: An Encyclopedia.* Mary B. Davis, editor. Pp.112-113.

Kroeber, Theodora
1961   *Ishi in Two Worlds: A Biography of the Last Wild Indian in North America.* University of California Press.

Laird, Carobeth
1975   *Encounter with an Angry God*. University of New Mexico Press.

Martinez, Wilton and Paul H. Gelles
1993   *Transnational Fiesta: 1992*. Film. Berkeley Media.
2013   *Transnational Fiesta: Twenty Years Later*. Film (in production).

Miller, Bruce
1988   *Chumash: A Picture of their World*. Sand River Press.

Mission Santa Ynez Website   www.missionsantaines.org

Norris, Jim.
2008   *Los Olivos*. Arcadia.

Raphael, Ray
2007   *Humboldt History: Two Peoples, One Place*. Freeman House.

Robbins, Catherine C.
2011   *All Indians Do Not Live in Teepees (or Casinos)*. University of Nebraska Press.

Robinson, Gary
2004   "Indian Governments and Indian Gaming: A Santa Ynez Chumash Perspective." An Educational booklet produced by Tribal Eye Productions.
2005   "The Samala People." DVD Film. An Educational Video produced by the Santa Ynez Band of Chumash Indians.
2007   "Tribal Sovereignty. The Right to Self-Rule." Tribal Eye Productions.
2008a   "Driving the Chumash Highway." *The California Indian* (7) 2:5-9.
2008b   "Those Who Defend Us." DVD Film. An Educational Video produced by the Santa Ynez Band of Chumash Indians.
2008c   *From Warriors to Soldiers: The History of Native American Service in the United States Military*. iUniverse.

2009   "Maria's Legacy." DVD Film. An Educational Video pro-
                duced by the Santa Ynez Band of Chumash Indians.

Sahlins, Marshall
2002   *Waiting for Foucault, Still.* Prickly Paradigm Press.

Sandoval, Nicolasa Irene
2007   *Bridging Generations: American Indian Family Perceptions of
                Home/School Partnerships.* PhD Dissertation: University of
                California at Santa Barbara.

Santa Ynez Band of Chumash Indians in Collaboration with Richard B.
                Applegate
2007   *Samala-English Dictionary.* Santa Ynez Band of Chumash
                Indians.

Santa Ynez Band of Chumash Indians Website   www.santaynezchumash.org

Santa Ynez Historical Calendar
2006   Santa Ynez Historical Calendar. Published by the Santa
                Ynez Historical Society.

Sherman Indian Museum Website   www.shermanindianmuseum.org

Smith, M.G.
1982   "The Nature and Variety of Plural Units." In *The Prospects for
                Plural Societies.* Edited by David Maybury Lewis. American
                Ethnological Society.

Spilde, Kate
2003a   "An Unfair Argument: How Indian Gaming Provides
                Benefits for California." *Global Gaming Business Magazine.*
2003b   "Creating a Political Space for American Indian Economic
                Development." *Local Actions: Cultural Activism, Power and
                Public Life in America*, Maggie Fishman   and Melissa
                Checker, editors. Columbia University Press.

2004   "Social and Economic Consequences of Indian Gaming in
            Oklahoma." *American Indian Culture and Research Journal*
            Vol. 28, No. 2.
2006   "Old Traditions, New Opportunities: Indian Gaming on
            the Pechanga Reservation." *American Behavioral Scientist.*

Spilde, K.A., J.B. Taylor, and K.W. Grant
2002   *Social and Economic Analysis of Tribal Government Gaming
            in Oklahoma.* The Harvard Project on American Indian
            Economic Development.

Starn, Orin
2004   *Ishi's Brain. In Search of America's Last "Wild" Indian.* New
            York: Norton.

Timbrook, Jan
2007   *Chumash Ethnobotany: Plant Knowledge Among the Chumash
            People of Southern California.* Heyday Books.

Tompkins, Walter A.
1982   *Stagecoach Days in Santa Barbara County.* McNally and
            Loftin.

Trafzer, Clifford E., Jean A. Keller, Lorene Sisquoc
2006   *Boarding school blues: Revisiting American Indian Educational
            Experiences.* Harcourt College Publishers.

Van Cott, Donna Lee, editor
1994   *Indigenous Peoples and Democracy in Latin America.* St. Martin's
            Press.

Walker, Phillip L. and John Johnson
1992   "Effects of Contact on the Chumash Indians." In *Disease
            and Demography in the Americas.* Edited by John Verano and
            Douglas Ubelaker. Smithsonian Institution Press.
1994   "The Decline of the Chumash Indian Population." In *Wake
            of Contact*, pp. 109-120. Wiley-Liss.

Weighill, Tharon
2002   "The 2-step tales of Hahashka: Experiences in Corporeality
              and Embodiment in Aboriginal California." Ph.D.
              Dissertation. University of California at Riverside.

Wheelright, Jane Hollister
1988   *The Ranch Papers: A California Memoir.* Lapis Press.

Index

Numbers in italic indicate illustrations.

Made in the USA
Columbia, SC
22 March 2022

58003081R00143